Excel 2021

A Complete Guide for Beginners to Learn about the Features, Functions, Tools, and Formulas of Microsoft Excel

Noah Smith

The information herein is offered for informational purposes solely and is universal as such. The presentation of the information is without a contract or any guarantee assurance.

The trademarks used are without any consent, and the publication of the trademark is without permission or backing by the trademark owner. All trademarks and brands within this book are for clarifying purposes only and are owned by the owners themselves, not affiliated with this document.

Table of Contents

Introduction

In the present-day world, the computer has proven to be a boon and has made it easy for us to do a lot of things that were a mere figment of one's imagination some years back.

With the changing times, tons of applications are developed by software developers in order to carry out various functions in the computer world.

One such application is Microsoft Excel, popularly called MS Excel.

This application has brought quite a revolution in the software world, as it has proved its worth in almost every field of work.

Microsoft Excel is a widely popular Microsoft Office program. It's a database software for saving and analyzing numerical results.

In this book, we'll go through the most critical aspects of MS Excel, an explanation of how to use it, its advantages, as well as other vital features.

The foundation of the book is a simple concept. To grasp the concept, you must devote as much time to planning as necessary. This will not only help you become a more capable user of Microsoft Excel, but it will also give you the confidence to use the software on your own, enabling you to create much more sophisticated programs capable of performing a variety of tasks.

Besides that, this book will not only assist you in mastering a new skill, namely a full understanding of Microsoft Excel, but it will also push you to practice enough to master this ability. So, basically, you'll be learning and practicing different concepts, functions, and formulas, that you'll use later in your social, professional, or academic life after you've finished your project or app.

Chapter 1: Microsoft Excel - Fundamental Know-How

1.1 What is MS Excel?

Microsoft Excel is a spreadsheet application for storing and analyzing numerical and mathematical data. Microsoft Excel includes a variety of resources for performing tasks such as equations, pivot tables, graphing tools, macro programming, and more. It works for a variety of operating systems, including Windows, Mac OS, Android, and iOS.

A table is created by a series of columns and rows in an Excel spreadsheet. Columns are customarily allocated alphabetical characters, while rows are typically assigned numbers. A cell is the intersection of a column and a row. A cell's address is determined by the letter that represents the column and the number that represents the row.

In Excel, data analysis is easy. The illustration below depicts the appearance of an Excel spreadsheet:

1.2 Microsoft Excel: Historical Background

Microsoft launched Multiplan in 1982, a spreadsheet software that was very popular on CP/M systems but lost ground on MS-DOS systems to Lotus 1-2-3.

The first Mac version of Excel was launched in 1985, and the first Windows edition was released in November 1987. (Numbered 2.0 to match the Mac and bundled with a run-time Windows environment.) Lotus took its time getting 1-2-3 to Windows, and by 1988, Excel had started to outsell 1-2-3, aiding Microsoft's rise to the top of the PC product market. This feat, which dethroned the software universe, founded Microsoft as a credible competitor and demonstrated the company's dedication to developing graphical software in the future. Through launching new applications every two years or so, Microsoft was able to retain its lead.

Excel was the subject of a trademark lawsuit early in its life by a company that was already selling a financial software kit named "Excel." As part of the case, Microsoft was required to refer to the app as "Microsoft Excel" in all public press releases and legal documents. However, this practice fell out of favor over time, and when Microsoft purchased the rights to the other software, the issue was finally settled. While it is no longer often used, Microsoft has encouraged the use of the letters XL as a shorthand for the program; the program's icon is still a stylized mixture of two letters, and the default Excel format's file extension is .xls.

While Excel has a more user-friendly interface than the first electronic spreadsheets, VisiCalc's nature remains the same: cells are organized in rows and columns and provide information or formulas with absolute, or relative references to other cells.

Excel was the first spreadsheet that let users change the presentation (fonts, cell appearance, and character attributes). Intelligent cell recomputation was also applied, which updates only the cells that are dependent on the cell that is being modified, (previously, spreadsheet programs would constantly recalculate all, or would wait for a particular user instruction). Excel has a number of graphing options.

When Microsoft Office was first released in 1993, the user interfaces for Microsoft Word and Microsoft PowerPoint were updated to work with Excel, the PC's killer app at the time.

Since 1993, Excel also included Visual Basic for Applications (VBA), a Visual Basic-based programming language that helps users to simplify activities in Excel and construct user-specific functions (UDF) for use in worksheets. VBA is a flexible extension to the program that, in later releases, offers a fully featured integrated application platform (IDE). Macro recording may produce VBA code that mimics user behavior, making task automation simple. VBA assists you in interacting with customers by allowing you to create forms and in-worksheet controls. Later variants of the language support class modules, allow basic object-oriented programming (OOP) methods. ActiveX (COM) DLLs may be used (but not created) in the language.

Because of VBA's automation capability, Excel has become a target for macro viruses. This was a big concern in the commercial world before antivirus products began to recognize these viruses. Microsoft eventually responded by allowing users to disable macros altogether, enable macros when opening a workbook, or trust all macros signed with a trusted certificate.

1.3 How to open Microsoft Excel?

Follow the steps below to open MS Excel on your computer:

1. Click on Start.

2. Then choose All Programs.

3. The next step is to open MS Office, for that, click on MS Office.

4. Finally, choose MS-Excel from the drop-down menu.

5. Alternatively, you can use the Start button and look for MS Excel in the open search box.

1.4 Main Purpose of MS Excel

Excel is a database software for saving, arranging, and editing numbers and data on a computer. It's an incredibly versatile software for figuring out responses to logic-based problems. It's a software that can organize a large amount of information into graphs and tables.

1.5 Things You Can Make in Excel

Outstanding. Long spreadsheets, complex macros, bar graphs, and the occasional pivot table, are likely to come to mind when you hear the term.

Excel has become the technical norm in offices around the world for pretty much everything that needs vast volumes of data handled, with more than almost one billion Microsoft Office users worldwide.

Think twice if you think Excel is only helpful in getting you cross-eyed when staring at a collection of numbers and financial records. Instead of basic spreadsheets, there are a variety of uses for Excel in the industry (and beyond), as Tomasz Tunguz pointed out. In truth, the potential benefits seem to be limitless.

We won't be able to compile a collection that includes all of Excel's potential programs (even if you're willing to read a listicle the size of War and Peace).

However, in order to show the strength and flexibility of everyone's favorite spreadsheet tool, we've compiled a list of different ways you should use Excel—both professionally and personally, as well as just for fun.

All About Numbers

For instance, Excel's primary function is to work with numbers. Excel allows sorting, retrieving, and analyzing a vast (or even minor) volume of data.

When it comes to using Excel for something numbers-related, there are a few different categories to bear in mind.

1. Calculating

2. Accounting

3. Chart

4. Inventory Tracking

Step by step, all points are discussed below.

1. Calculating

Do you ever find yourself doing the same calculations? By programming your frequently used calculations in Excel, you will build a fully personalized calculator. That way, all you have to do is punch in your numbers, and Excel will calculate the response for you—no effort needed.

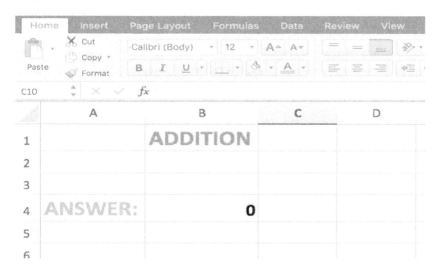

2. Accounting

Budgeting, forecasting, cost monitoring, financial reporting, loan calculators, and other tools are all accessible. Excel was essentially created to meet these various accounting requirements. And, given that 89% of businesses use Excel for multiple accounting functions, it clearly meets the criteria.

Excel also comes with a variety of spreadsheet models to help you with these tasks.

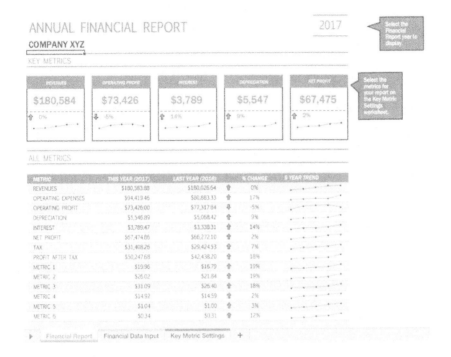

3. Charts

The number of pie charts, line charts, scatter charts, region charts, bar charts, and column charts is endless. Excel's ability to turn rows and columns of digits into stunning charts is sure to become one of your favorite features if you need to represent data in a more visual and easily understandable way.

Want to learn more about the different kinds of charts you can make in Excel? This book is an excellent resource.

Budget

% of Income Spent Summary

Total Monthly Income
$3,750

Total Monthly Expenses
$2,058

Total Monthly Savings
$550

Cash Balance
$1,142

55%

4. Inventory Tracking

Inventory tracking can be a pain. Fortunately, Excel will assist employees, company owners, and even people, in staying prepared and on top of their inventory.

Personal Inventory

Name	Insurance Company	Agent Address
[Name]	[Company]	[Address]
Address	Agent	Agent Phone
[Address]	[Name]	[Phone/Fax]
Phone	Company Phone	Agent Email
[Phone]	[Phone]	[Email]
Email	Policy Number	
[Email]	[Policy]	

Item Description	Category	Serial Number	Value
[Item]	[Category]	[Serial #]	[Value]
[Item]	[Category]	[Serial #]	[Value]
[Item]	[Category]	[Serial #]	[Value]
[Item]	[Category]	[Serial #]	[Value]
[Item]	[Category]	[Serial #]	[Value]
[Item]	[Category]	[Serial #]	[Value]
[Item]	[Category]	[Serial #]	[Value]
[Item]	[Category]	[Serial #]	[Value]
Total			$0.00

Making a Plan

Let's get away from the numbers for a moment—Excel will help you schedule and arrange a variety of things that don't need infinite rows of digits. These are:

1. Calendars and Schedules

2. Seating Charts

3. Goal Planning Worksheet

4. Mock-ups

1. Calendars and Schedules

Do you need to build a content schedule for your blog or website? Are you looking for lesson plans for your school environment? Is there a PTO routine for you and your co-workers? Do you or your family have a regular schedule? Excel can be handy when it comes to varying calendars and schedules.

Daily Schedule							
Week: [Date] Start Time: 5:00 AM							
	Mon	Tue	Wed	Thu	Fri	Sat	Sun
5:00 AM		Go to gym					
5:30 AM							
6:00 AM							
6:30 AM							
7:00 AM							
7:30 AM							
8:00 AM							
8:30 AM							
9:00 AM							

2. Seating Charts

Creating a seating chart for everything from an extensive business luncheon to a reception may be a royal pain. Excel, fortunately, will render things a breeze. If you are an absolute whiz, you will be able to generate your seating chart automatically from your RSVP spreadsheet.

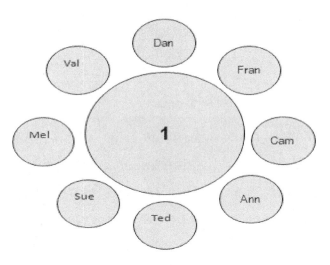

3. Worksheet for Goal Planning

It helps to have something to keep you centered and on track, whether it's career goals, health goals, or financial goals. You can use the app to build a variety of worksheets, logs, even planning papers to track your success and, ideally, reach the finish line.

Task	Times/Week	S	M	T	W	T	F	S	Complete
Go for a run	2	✔		✔					Yay!
Don't Leave Dirty Dishes Overnight	2	✔			✔		✔		Yay!
Eat 1 Fruit or Vegetable	3	✔			✔	✔	✔	✔	Yay!
Floss	3	✔		✔			✔	✔	Yay!

8-3-2014

Task	Times/Week	S	M	T	W	T	F	S	Complete
Go for a run	2								0 of 2
Don't Leave Dirty Dishes Overnight	3								0 of 3
Eat 1 Fruit or Vegetable	3								0 of 3
Floss	3								0 of 3

8-10-2014

Task	Times/Week	S	M	T	W	T	F	S	Complete
Go for a run	3								0 of 3
Don't Leave Dirty Dishes Overnight	3								0 of 3
Eat 1 Fruit or Vegetable	4								0 of 4
Floss	4								0 of 4

8-17-2014

Task	Times/Week	S	M	T	W	T	F	S	Complete
Go for a run	3								0 of 3
Don't Leave Dirty Dishes Overnight	3								0 of 3
Eat 1 Fruit or Vegetable	5								0 of 5
Floss	4								0 of 4

4. Mock-ups

When it comes to programming, Excel may not be the first thing that comes to mind. However, believe it or not, the platform can be used to create different mock-ups and designs. It's a standard option for designing website wireframes and dashboards.

Getting Stuff Done

Do you want to increase your productivity? Excel will come to the rescue with a multitude of functions that can help you manage your activities and to-dos with ease and organization.

1. Task List

2. Check List

3. Project Management Charts

4. Time Logs

1. Task List

Say goodbye to the old-fashioned to-do list on paper. With Excel, you can create a much more comprehensive task list, and also track your performance on the more significant tasks you already have on your plate.

TASK LIST					
MY TASKS	START DATE	DUE DATE	% COMPLETE	DONE	NOTES
[Task]	[Date]	[Date]	0%		
[Task]	[Date]	[Date]	50%		
[Task]	[Date]	[Date]	100%	●	

2. Checklist

Similarly, you could make a quick checklist to cross off the items you've bought or completed—from a shopping list, to a list of to-dos for a future marketing campaign.

PURCHASED?	GROCERIES:
☐	Apples
☐	Tomatoes
☐	Milk
☐	Eggs
☐	Cheese
☐	Bread

3. Project Management Charts

Excel is a complete beast when it comes to making charts, as we've already mentioned. This principle remains when it comes to project management charts.

Excel will aid you in keeping your project on track in a variety of ways, from waterfall charts to Kanban-style boards (like Trello), to monitor your team's progress.

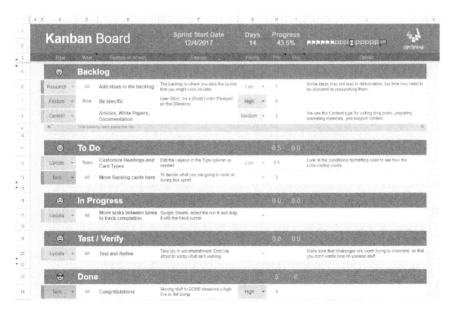

4. Time Logs

Keeping track of your time has been known to help you be more productive. Although there are several fancy applications and software's to help you fulfill the need, think of Excel as the initial time-tracking application. It continues to be a viable alternative today.

Involving Other People

Do you need to gather information from others? One choice is to use survey tools and forms. Still, don't worry; you can make your own in Excel.

1. Forms

2. Quizzes

1. Forms

Excel is a beautiful tool for creating forms, from basic to complex. You can also program different drop-down menus so users can choose from a pre-defined assortment of options.

2. Quizzes

Are you trying to assess someone else's — or even your own — understanding of a subject? You can build a bank of questions and answers in one worksheet and then have Excel quiz you in another.

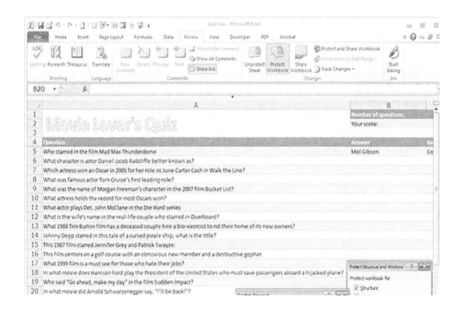

Staying in Touch

Relationship management is vital to your professional and personal growth. Excel, fortunately, makes it easy to stay in contact.

1. CRM

2. Mailing List

1. CRM

If you need a simple CRM to keep top-of-mind for your clients? One can be generated in Excel. What's more, the best part? It would be fully flexible if you create it yourself. To support you in getting started, Sales Hacker has put together a handy series of free sales excel templates.

CRM Template
[Your Name]

Name	Company	Work Function	Phone	Email	Estimated Sale	Last Contact	Next Action	Next Contact	Lead Status	Lead Source	Notes
Jameson, Bill	XYZ Plumbing	Owner	444-555-6666	xyz@plumber.com	$ 45,000	1/10/13		1/29/13	Cold	Referral	
Anderson, Jane	ABC Corp	Sales Manager	222-656-7890	busi@abccorp.com	$ 10,000	1/25/13		2/5/13	Warm	Website	
Smithers, Joe	ACME	Business Dev.	111-234-5678	acme@acme.com	$ 4,500	1/27/13		2/15/13	Active	Email	Loves chocolate

Insert new rows above the gray line

2. Mailing List

Data does not always have to be numerical. Excel is also excellent at handling and sorting vast lists of names and addresses, making it ideal for the company's holiday party invitation list, or the mailing list for a significant promotion or campaign.

	A	B	C	D	E	F
1	FIRST NAME	LAST NAME	ADDRESS	CITY	STATE	ZIP CODE
2	Oprah	Winfrey	123 Magnificent Mile Ave.	Chicago	IL	58922
3	Mister	Rodgers	8935 Beautiful Day Rd.	New York	NY	23935
4	Hulk	Hogan	9284 Hollywood Blvd.	Los Angeles	CA	39825

You may also mail combine using Excel, which makes printing address labels and other resources a lot simpler.

It can also be used to build folders, RSVP lists, & other rosters that provide a lot of information about individuals.

Having Fun

It doesn't have to be all work and no play when it comes to Excel. You can make a variety of other interesting items with the spreadsheet tool.

1. Historical Logs

2. Sudoku Puzzles

3. Word Cloud

4. Art and animations

5. Trip planner

1. Historical Logs

If you'd like to keep track of the different craft drinks you've tried, the exercises you've done, or anything else entirely, Excel will help you keep it organized and logged.

Workout Log

Stats

Average Duration (minutes)	Average Calories
35	402

Average Distance (miles/km)	Average Weight
2.75	131

Average Pace (per hour)
4.88

Workouts

DATE	ACTIVITY	DURATION (minutes)	DISTANCE (miles/km)	PACE (per hour)	CALORIES	WEIGHT	NOTES
8/18/17	Cross Trainer	40	2.50	3.75	380	132	[Notes]
8/20/17	Treadmill	30	3.00	6.00	423	130	[Notes]

2. Sudoku puzzles

Do you like Sudoku puzzles? As it turns out, you can make your own in Excel,. Alternatively, if you're stuck on an especially difficult one, you may enlist the support of Excel to help you work it out!

	A	B	C	D	E	F	G	H	I	J
1					1	7				
2	4						5			
3			9							
4						1		9		
5			5	7	8					
6	1			2					6	
7	5		4		2				3	
8	2				3	8		6	4	
9		1	3			9		5		

3. Word cloud

Word clouds aren't the most scientific way to view results. They are, though, an enjoyable (not to mention beautiful), way to learn about the most commonly used words. You guessed it— Excel can be used to create one. It's possible to make a word cloud in Wordle using data from Excel.

Edit Language Font Layout Color

Cake
Brownies
Squares Pie
Tarts
Cookies

4. Art and animations

Excel's features are sure to go well beyond what you would expect. Most people have used tools to create some really fantastic artwork, ranging from pixelated images to animations.

5. Trip Planner

Do you have a holiday planned? Before you grab your bags and go, make sure you have it covered by making a handy itinerary. You can also use Excel to create a trip planner framework to ensure you don't forget something (from your budget to airline details).

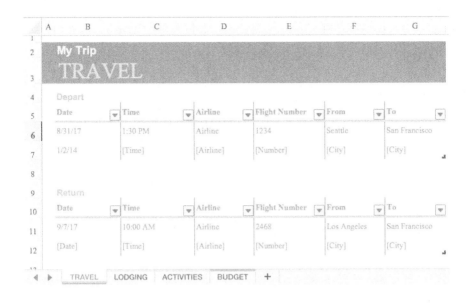

1.6 Top 10 Features of MS Excel

The following are the top 10 Excel features: -

1. Pivot Tables

They're used to sort, count, sum, or average data, from a single spreadsheet and show it in a new chart, allowing you to cut and paste as required. That is the most critical aspect of this feature. It's simple to limit the search to revenue numbers for individual regions, product categories, or marketing platforms. This way, you can ensure that the data is free of errors.

2. Add Multiple Rows

Perhaps it is one of the most often-performed spreadsheet operations. The shortcut is Ctrl-Shift +, but it takes a while, so we suggest Right Click instead. If you choose to add more than one, pick the desired number of columns or rows, then Right Click and then Add.

3. Print Optimisation

Printing can be a pain for all. Imagine that anything you printed was just what you wanted to print. It is, in fact, feasible. Print preview, changing margins, fit to one page, print selection, portrait vs. landscape, printing headers, and spreadsheet-style are all things to consider. Spend the time to get acquainted with it. This is a role that you will do several times in your career.

4. Flash Fill

In 2013, Excel created its own unique personality. Let's just assume you have two columns of names and need to generate email addresses from both of them. Simply do that for the first row, and Excel will figure out what you're talking about and complete the rest for you. This was feasible prior to 2013, but it required a variety of steps.

5. Filters

Quickly explore data in a table. Filtering effectively masks non-interesting results. Typically, if you're aiming for a specific value, such as "blue vehicles," filters would highlight those and conceal the others. However, you can now filter on number values (e.g., is more significant than, highest 10%, etc.), and cell color in more recent iterations of Excel. Where you need to filter more than one column at the same time, such as both colors and vehicles, to locate your blue car, filtering becomes more efficient.

6. Conditional Formatting

Conditional formatting, when used correctly, brings out the patterns of the world as recorded by the spreadsheet. This has the potential to be sophisticated. Also, the color changes, though simple, may be beneficial. Assume that the sales department sells a certain amount of product per month. In only three clicks, you will discover the top 10% of salespeople and start a fruitful market discussion.

7. Paste Special

One of the more popular Excel tasks is grabbing (or copying) data from one cell and pasting it into another. However, there is a lot you might want to copy (formatting, formula, value, comments, etc.), and you might not want to copy anything. The most popular scenario is where you try to remove the formatting and save the data to your own spreadsheet using your own composition.

8. Absolute References

Unavoidable! F4 toggles between the four possible variations by placing a dollar in front of the letter and a dollar sign in front of the figure.

9. Extend formula across/down

Excel's scalability is one of the most appealing features. Excel can spit out the correct equation a million times if you have the formula correct the first time. The + crosshair is really useful. If you have continuous results, double-clicking it will carry it all the way down. You will find that copying and pasting (either standard paste or paste formulas) is more accessible.

10. Index-match

It is one of the most effective Excel role combinations. It can be used to look up a value in a large table of data and then return a value in that table. Let's assume your organization has 10K workers, and you have a spreadsheet with all their records, including salaries, start date, line manager, and so on. However, you have a staff of 20 people, and you're only involved in them. This will look up the importance of your team members in the table (these must be special, such as an email address or an employee number) and display the desired details for the team. It's worth taking your time to get your mind around this because it's more versatile and efficient than VLOOKUPs.

1.7 Simplified Features of MS Excel

An Excel spreadsheet can be edited and formatted in a variety of ways. The different features of MS Excel are discussed below.

The composition of features in MS Excel is seen in the picture below:

1. Home

Comprises options like font styles, font size, font color, alignment, background color, formatting options and styles, deletion and insertion of cells, and editing options.

Data

This group includes features such as adding additional data (from the web), search options, and data resources.

2. Insert

Inserting photos and numbers, table format and layout, adding diagrams, maps, and sparklines, equation and symbol choices, and header and footer options are all included in this tab.

3. Review

In the review category, proofreading (like spell check), can be performed on an excel document, and a reader can add notes in this section.

4. Page Layout

The page layout tab includes choices for themes, alignment, and page configuration.

5. View

This is where we can adjust the views under which the spreadsheet is viewed. This segment contains options for zooming in and out, as well as pane layout.

6. Formulas

Since MS Excel can generate tables with a vast volume of details, you can use this function to apply formulas to the table and get faster results.

1.8 Understanding the Ribbon

In Excel, the ribbon gives shortcuts to commands. A command is an action taken by the operator. Creating a fresh text, printing a document, and so on, are examples of commands. The ribbon in Excel 2013 is seen in the picture below.

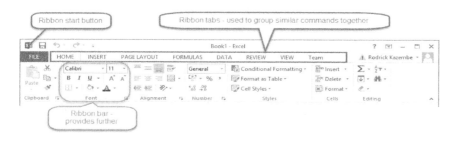

Components of the ribbon are defined under:

- **The start button of Ribbon**– The start button of ribbon is used to approach commands such as creating new documents, printing, saving existing work, & using Excel's customization choices, among others.

- **Ribbon bar** – this bar is used to group commands that are identical. The Alignment ribbon bar, for example, is used to organize all the commands that are used to align data together.

- **Ribbon tabs** – this tab is used to group commands that are identical. Basic commands like formatting data to make it more presentable, sorting and searching unique data inside the spreadsheet are performed on the home page.

Getting to Know the Worksheet (Rows and Columns, Workbooks, Sheets)

- **A workbook is a collection of worksheets.** A workbook in Excel has three cells by default. To meet your needs, you can erase or add more sheets. Sheet1, Sheet2, and so on, are the default names for the covers. You should rename the sheets to something more important, like Daily Expenses or Monthly Budget, etc.

- **A worksheet is a collection of columns and rows**. A cell is formed when a row and a column intersect. Data is recorded in cells. A cell address is used to identify each cell individually. Letters are used to mark columns, and numbers are used to label rows.

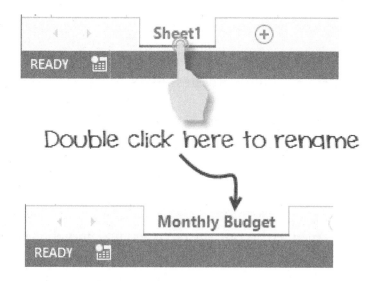

Microsoft Excel Environment Customization

You do not want to use ribbon tabs such as developer if you are not a programmer, however, you can change the theme color as per your liking. Any of this is possible thanks to customizations. We'll look at the following sub-sections.

1. Customization of ribbon

2. Settings for formulas

3. Proofing settings

4. Setting the color theme

5. Save settings

1. Customization of ribbon

The default ribbon in Excel 2013 is seen in the picture above. Let's start with the ribbon customization. Let's say you don't want to see any of the tabs on the toolbar, or you want to include some missing tabs, such as the developer tab. You can do this by using the options window.

- To begin, click the ribbon's start button.

- From the drop-down screen, choose your options. You must be able to see a dialogue box called Excel Options.

- As seen below, select the customize ribbon option from the left side screen.

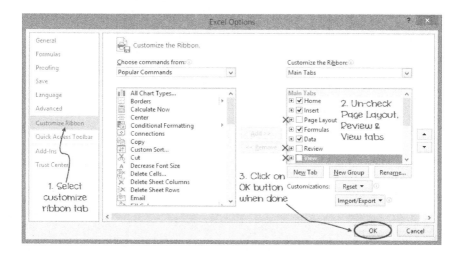

- Delete the checkmarks from the buttons from the right side that you don't want to see on the ribbon. We have removed the Review, Page Layout, and View tabs for this illustration.

- When you're done, click the "OK" icon.

Your ribbon will look as follows

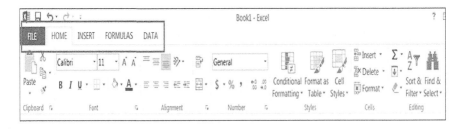

Adding custom tabs to the ribbon

You may also create your own page, name it whatever you want, and delegate its commands. Let's make a tab with the text Guru99 in the ribbon.

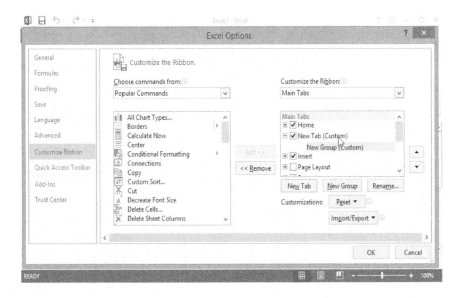

- Select Customize the Ribbon from the menu bar when you right-click on the ribbon. A discussion window similar to the one seen above will appear.

- As seen in the animated picture, click the new tab icon.

- Choose the newly added column.

- Rename the file by clicking the Rename icon.

- Give it the name Guru99.

- As seen in the image, go to the Guru99 tab and select New Group (Custom).

- Rename it My Commands by clicking the Rename icon.

- Let's go ahead and apply those commands to my ribbon bar.

- On the middle panel, you'll find a list of commands.

- Select the command 'All chart' categories and then press the Add icon.

- Select OK.

2. Settings for formulas

You may use this option to monitor how Excel acts when working with formulas. It may be used to modify options such as autocomplete while entering formulas, changing the cell referencing type, and using numbers for both columns and rows, among other things.

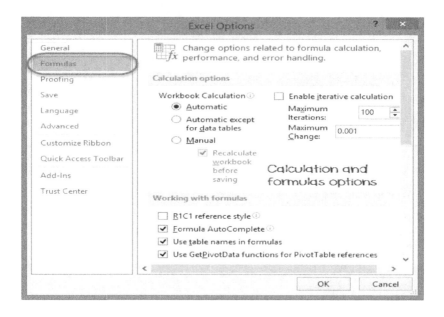

To make an option available, click a button next to it. Remove the checkmark from the checkbox to deactivate an alternative. This customization is available in the Options dialogue box, under the Formulas tab on the left-hand side column.

3. Proofing settings

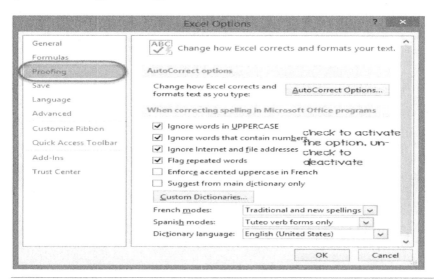

This option alters the text that has been entered into Excel. It helps you customize things like the dictionary language that can be used while searching for misspellings, dictionary tips, and so on. This customatization is available in the options dialogue window on the left-hand side column, under the proofing tab.

4. Setting the color theme

To change the color theme of an Excel board, go to the Excel ribbon and select the file option command. It will open the window where you must complete the steps below.

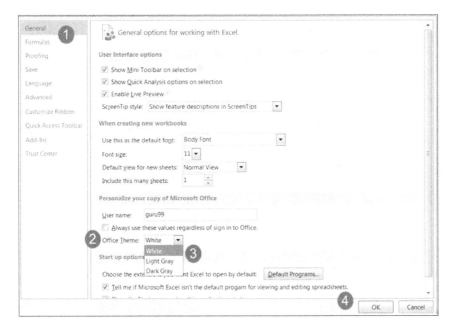

- By default, the general tab on the left-hand side would be chosen.

- Look under the General options for dealing in Excel for a color scheme.

- Select the appropriate color from the color scheme drop-down column.

- Select the OK tab.

5. Save settings

This feature enables you to set the default file format while saving data, as well as permit auto recovery in the event that your computer shuts down before you can save your work. This choice is available in the Options dialogue window, under the Save tab on the left-hand side screen.

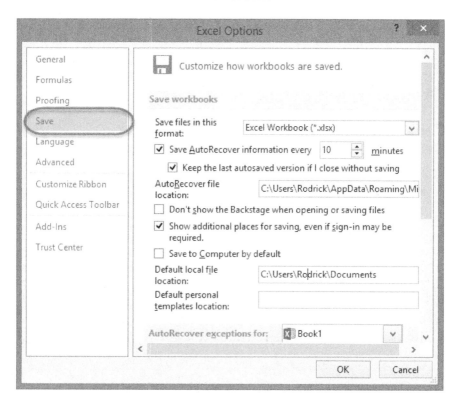

Chapter 2: Uses of MS Excel

Microsoft Excel is commonly used these days by all because it is beneficial and saves time. It has been in operation for several years and is updated with new functionality every year. MS Excel's most remarkable feature is that it can be used everywhere for almost any kind of work. It's used for things like accounting, data processing, analysis, procurement, financing, company tasks, and complicated calculations, among other things. It may also be used to perform statistical calculations and to store valuable data in the form of spreadsheets or charts.

Microsoft Excel protects the archives, ensuring that no one else can access or corrupt them. You can password-protect your data with the aid of Microsoft Excel. Microsoft Excel can be downloaded from any location and at any time. If you don't have access to a desktop, you are able to use your phone to operate on Excel. Microsoft Excel has so many advantages that it has become an unavoidable feature of millions of people's lives. It has a variety of resources and characteristics that render it more manageable and saves time.

The ten most effective uses of Microsoft Excel are as follows:

2.1 Storing and analyzing data

One of the most valuable features of Excel is the ability to analyze vast volumes of data in order to spot patterns. You can summarise data and archive it in an orderly manner with the aid of graphs and maps so that you can quickly access it anytime you need it. It becomes simpler to store records, and you can save a lot of time as a result.

Data may be utilized for a variety of applications until it has been stored in a structured manner. MS Excel allows a person to easily perform different operations on data by including a variety of resources.

2.2 Spreadsheets and data recovery

Another prominent characteristic of Excel is that if the data is corrupted, you can quickly regain it. If a person in business has valuable data saved in Excel and it is missing, or the file is destroyed, he need not fear since the new MS Excel XML format will be used to recover the lost or broken file data.

Another significant application is that Excel spreadsheets render your task more accessible, and you can lessen the size of the spreadsheet and make things manageable in a more timely manner with the current Microsoft Excel XML format.

2.3 Security

The essential aspect of MS Excel is that it secures Excel archives, allowing users to keep their data protected. Via simple visual programming or directly inside the excel file, all MS Excel files can be password-protected. People keep their valuable data in MS Excel so that they can keep it organised, safe, and it saves them time.

Almost everybody needs their data to be password locked so that no one may access them or destroy them, and MS Excel is an excellent solution to this issue.

2.4 Online access

Another quality of MS Excel is that it can be downloaded electronically from anywhere and at any time, allowing you to use it from any device and place. It will enable you to function more conveniently, which ensures even if you don't have a laptop, you can use your phone to complete your tasks quickly and effectively. As a result of the extensive versatility that MS Excel offers, people can use it regardless of their technology and venue.

2.5 Helps businesspeople in developing future strategy

Data may be represented in the form of charts and graphs to aid in the identification of various patterns. Trend lines may be expanded beyond the graph with the aid of MS Excel, making it far simpler to analyze trends and patterns. In order to increase profits, it is crucial to evaluate the appeal of products or the selling trend that they adopt. MS Excel makes this challenge easier for company owners, allowing them to flourish and increase earnings.

2.6 Excel tools make your work easier

MS Excel has a plethora of resources that not only makes the job a lot easier ,but saves time. There are fantastic resources for sorting, browsing, and scanning, that make the job much easier. You will complete the job in even less time if you mix these methods with scales, pivot tables, and other tools. Multiple components can be conveniently included in vast volumes of data to assist in the resolution of a variety of issues and queries.

2.7 Mathematical formulas make things easier

The very best use of MS Excel is that it allows you to solve complicated mathematical problems in a much easier and less time-consuming manner. There are several formulas in MS Excel, and by using them, you will perform a variety of operations on a vast volume of data at once, such as finding the sum, average, and so on. As a result, MS Excel is used anytime people need to solve complicated mathematical problems, or add essential mathematical functions to tables with lots of detail.

2.8 Sophisticated data presentations

Another strength of Microsoft Excel is that it allows you to bring more sophistication to the data presentations, which ensures you can refine the data bars, highlight any relevant things you wish to stress, and efficiently make the data more presentable.

If you have data stored in Excel and you wish to illustrate something significant, you can do so using the different data presentation features included in MS Excel. One might also create spreadsheets based on which one can process data more appealingly.

2.9 Store data together at one location

Another helpful feature of MS Excel is that it allows you to have all your data in one place. This will assist you in preventing the loss of your records. It will keep all the data together in one place, so you won't have to spend time looking for files. As a result, you can save time and will be able to quickly look up the sorted and categorized data anytime you need it.

2.10 Manage expenditure

MS Excel is helpful for budgeting. For example, if a person earns $50k per month, he would incur certain costs, and if he needs to know precisely how much he is paying per month, he will quickly do so with Excel. He will enter his monthly revenue and expenditures into excel tables, which will enable him to see how much he is spending and, as a result, monitor it.

To conclude, these are only some advantages of using MS Excel, which is why it is used by people all over the world for a variety of activities. Not only can it save resources, but it also helps make the job simpler. It is almost capable of doing any task. For, e.g., you can perform quantitative calculations as well as create graphs and charts to store data. It is easy for a businessperson to quantify and store data in it.

MS Excel has the ability to store and interpret vast amounts of data. It helps to hold all the details in one location so that nothing is missed and no time is wasted looking for specific information.

Chapter 3: Merits and Demerits of using MS Excel

Microsoft Excel, also known as Ms-Excel or simply Excel, is a versatile application program created by Microsoft as part of the Microsoft Office Suite for Android, Windows, macOS, and iOS.

The working group uses the application, and it reads Microsoft Office Suite for calculations, collating data and details, simulation, and so on.

However, because of the value and advantage of obtaining a working knowledge of Excel in an era of rapid technological development, it is now taught to students, particularly in high school, through computer science courses.

As the environment becomes increasingly data-driven, Ms-Excel is one of the programs that provides us with resources to help us work with data in innovative ways. Still, in the end, we cannot argue that the data we're dealing with isn't limited to 100 rows & 100 columns, but rather tens of thousands.

As a result, Ms-Excel has drawbacks that we cannot ignore while considering its use. In this post, we will look at different parts of Microsoft Excel in order to get a better understanding of it and make an informed decision.

3.1 Merits of Using MS Excel

1. Simple and powerful comparisons

If you have been in the financial sector for a while, you are already aware of how frequently comparisons are made to explain how the stock market changes.

Not only in business, but also in psychology, sociology, and political science, professionals often compare data to explain trends in their study, such as political data, how caste and family income interacted in the past and present, and so on.

Microsoft Excel provides you with the opportunity to examine vast amounts of data and discover patterns that can affect the outcome of the work you've been doing due to the strong analytical tools used.

Data analysis techniques such as tables, histograms, and box-plot charts are among the tools available. These tools assist you in analyzing and structuring the data without the added complexity of doing it manually using pen and paper.

2. Collaboration and accessibility

Through advancement in technology, Microsoft also produced a web version of their Office Suite software. This helps you to collaborate on the web version of Microsoft Excel with your friends or colleagues, allowing you and your peers to view and control the Excel database from everywhere at the same time.

As a result, if you are dealing with vast collections of data and get confused, you don't have to wait for the next meeting with a friend or colleague to get support.

Additionally, Microsoft has created Excel applications that can be built into devices, allowing users to display, update, and share Excel files.

Although Microsoft Excel is modified on a regular basis, the consumer may need the most up-to-date technologies to get the most out of it. This does not, however, prevent the consumer from using the program on a low-power PC or laptop.

3. Data and Analysis

Excel is an excellent tool for data processing, not just because it allows one to store data and execute calculations, but also because it contains a number of useful resources.

Filtering, sorting, and search methods are both powerful and easy ways to improve the user's capacity to easily narrow down the parameters when making decisions. As a result, the consumer can efficiently play with a large volume of data.

As a result, the added benefit of tables, pivot tables, and a variety of visualization methods, when paired with the above resources, will assist the user in quickly locating knowledge, despite a large number of data objects.

3.2 Demerits of Using MS Excel

1. Protection and Security

The data and information we are subjected to can be very wide at times. When a file is so big, the interpreter/compiler must go through every row and column, making the Excel program run slowly. Cutting down the file into smaller files is the simplest way to ensure Excel is time-efficient. However, certain details could be missing or misplaced as a result of this.

In addition, Microsoft Excel uses imprecise calculations to approximate very big quantities. As a result, accuracy is compromised, and the user has no control over the situation since this functionality is built-in.

As a result, if several people handle the same file's input, the file is prone to mistakes and inaccuracy. These errors are not only difficult to spot later in the process, but they may also have a negative impact on the bottom line.

2. Data and Development

It's safe to conclude that Microsoft Excel is an excellent method for doing a one-time analysis at this stage. This, though, may not always be the case.

Microsoft Excel is widely used in the business world, and like every business, you're always looking for ways to improve. The data expands and changes over time. As a result, you need a data tracking tool that can evolve with you. Excel, on the other hand, does not do any better in this regard.

To put it another way, the size of your company grows in direct relation to the amount of Excel spreadsheets you have, which stretches out the data more. As a consequence, it becomes difficult for the organization/user to keep up, which can contribute to poor outcomes and decisions.

3. Ineffective use of time

The data does not appear in the spreadsheet. Each and every detail must be entered manually by the consumer.

As a result, particularly if you have a large volume of data, it may take a long time, rendering Excel ineffective in terms of time performance. Often, since most people can only be vigilant for a limited amount of time, entering a large amount of data may contribute to errors.

To conclude, from its advantages and disadvantages, Excel's performance is dependent on the type of task the user wants to complete. Excel is an excellent method for quickly analyzing the data that the user has. However, if the data is critical to an organization's potential success, it might not be the ideal tool for dealing with other types of data.

Chapter 4: Innovative Tools of MS Excel

In today's workplace, the spreadsheet has unquestionably been one of the most important tools. It's difficult to imagine how we'd deal with data without the ability to organize it as efficiently as Excel enables.

Excel and Google Sheets are two of the most common structured data solutions on the market. They are at the cutting edge of functionality, allowing businesses to operate more efficiently and effectively. Businesses increase efficiency and add order to a variety of data forms through their assistance–using complicated formulas and charts, diagrams, and records.

Excel and Google Sheets are unquestionably powerful platforms, which is why we still need them. They can be difficult and clumsy to use at the same time. That's why it's worthwhile to investigate the most cutting-edge add-ons and add-ins that will aid you in becoming more efficient.

4.1 New in prosumer structured data tools

Spreadsheets will help you increase efficiency in a variety of industries. Though their strengths are impressive, businesses are continually in search of innovative approaches to deal with

their data in order to get the best out of it. That is why software developers create add-ons and additional tools that extend the capabilities of well-known spreadsheet programs.

Hundreds of thousands of additional Google Sheets and Excel resources are available, but not all of them can benefit your company. However, once you find the best, and most compatible extensions, they will make a huge difference in the team's productivity. They will save a lot of time that would otherwise be wasted on boring and routine activities. Many add-ons are inexpensive and easy to set up.

4.2 Innovative Tools for Spreadsheets

Open as App

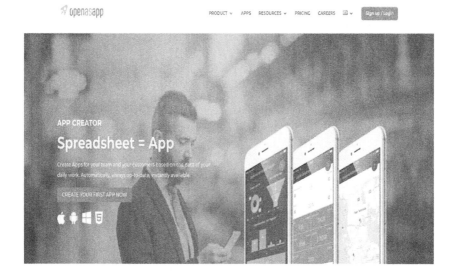

'Open as App' is a no-code app creator that allows you to make the most of your company results. It helps you quickly build applications from your spreadsheets with little effort and little technological knowledge. You can create applications that execute calculations using logic from your spreadsheet, which is wholly transferable and accessible. The great thing regarding 'Open as App' is that it can be used in conjunction with other Google Sheets add-ons to expand their functionality much more.

With only a few taps, you can build efficient applications from your Google Sheets or Excel spreadsheets.

Translate My Sheet

'Translate My Sheet' is a Google add-on that will provide you with translations for your spreadsheet texts in over 100 languages automatically. You may either convert a specific selection from a sheet or the whole sheet. When you first launch the add-on, you have the option of letting it pick the root language for you, or you can choose it yourself. After that, you must select the target language.

The main feature is that spreadsheets are automatically translated.

You can use 'Translate My Sheet' in conjunction with 'Open as App' to build multilingual apps. Translate the sheet first. Then save the app in the original language and paste it onto the translation sheet. 'Translate My Sheet' works well, but empty or connected cells should be avoided. You must remove them before using the add-on; otherwise, they may stop functioning.

Power Tools

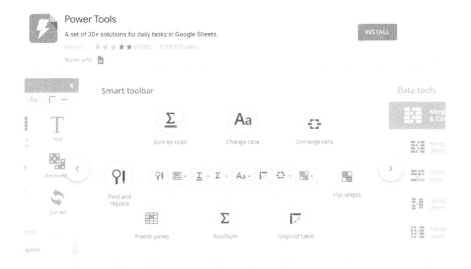

Power Tools is a collection of over 30 tools that can help you manage spreadsheets more quickly and easily. It can remove duplicates, merge cells, replace data, and import ranges from different sheets, among other things.

The main attribute of this is that there are 30 exclusive features that help you save time in spreadsheets by automating routine activities.

Pro tip: You should organize your spreadsheet with Power Tools, making it far simpler to build your custom software with 'Open as App' later.

Lucid chart Diagrams

In spreadsheets, Lucid chart diagrams give you the opportunity to make flowcharts and diagrams. It's a visual workspace that you can use to supplement the information in your Google Sheets or Excel documents.

The main attribute is that charts and graphs will help you visualize data from your spreadsheets.

Icons from Flat icon

'Flaticon' is the world's most prominent icon archive, with a G Suite plugin that includes Google Sheets. It provides individual vector icons as well as complete icon sets. You would use 'Flaticon' to render the spreadsheets simpler to understand by visualizing portions of the details in them.

The main attribute is: Obtain a more visually appealing spreadsheet with the use of icons.

'Flaticon' may be used in conjunction with 'Open as App'. Hover your mouse over the tiny icon preview, right-click, pick 'copy image source,' and paste it into your sheet's image column. When you're online, the icon will appear in the app. 'Flaticon' is a browser-dependent plugin that runs in Google Chrome.

Geocode by Awesome Table

'Geocode by awesome table' derives latitudes and longitudes from addresses in a Google Spreadsheet. It then positions them on a Google map so you can share quickly.

The main attribute is: In a spreadsheet, maps for addresses are shown.

Pro tip: You can only look at the map if you're connected to the internet. You'll need to do a few formatting improvements to use it for 'Open as App', but then you're good to go.

Form Approvals

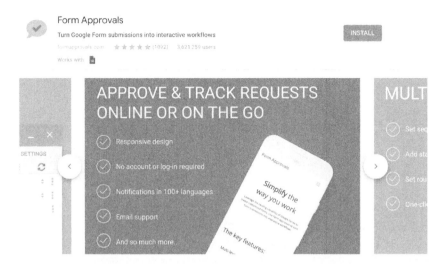

'Form Approvals' is a Google Forms add-on. You can use it to simplify processes by converting form inputs into immersive workflows. In a Google Sheet, the information obtained in the form is presented.

The main attribute is: Streamline the data collection and analysis of form submissions.

Pro tip: You can quickly convert a Google Sheet with your form's answer data into an app with 'Open as App', which includes a helpful map dashboard. The software will periodically upgrade when you receive further responses from the forms.

Sheet to Calendar Evento

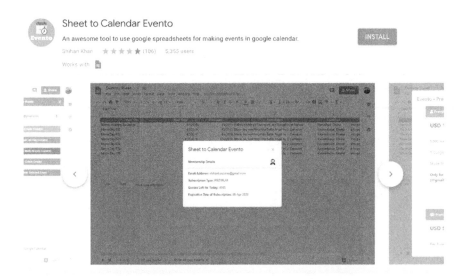

You can build Google Calendar events from the data in your Google Sheets using the add-on 'Sheet to Calendar Evento'. It populates the case with information from the spreadsheet. When you make changes to the sheet, the case is immediately changed.

The main attribute is: Create activities in Google Calendar in bulk using your spreadsheet.

Recommendation: You can stretch Evento's capabilities much more with 'Open as App'. You are able to make an event app from a spreadsheet by entering information regarding each event, such as the schedule and attendees.

XL Miner Analysis Tool Pak

'Analysis Tool Pak' for Excel is similar to 'XL Miner Analysis Tool Pak'. It has mathematical analysis features, including all 19 interactive functions from the Excel tool, as well as one more–logic regression.

The main attribute is: Statistical reporting capabilities that are more often used.

Pro tip: You can use 'Open as App' to build an app based on the calculations you make with 'XLMiner'. It can be used for the most popular formulas.

Google Analytics

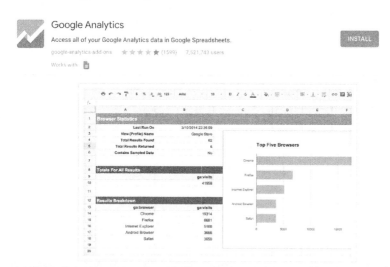

Google Analytics, one of the most well-known Google apps, can be used with Sheets. You can export any of your Analytics data to a spreadsheet with this add-on. This enables you to effectively scan and organize data in order to gain market insights.

The main attribute is: Data from Google Analytics can be accessed through your spreadsheets.

Recommendation: Use your Google Analytics data in a spreadsheet file, it's simple to create an account with 'Open as App'. This is how you can look over the data with the help of helpful dashboards and visualizations.

Bottleneck Detector

This tool aids in the removal of segments from the Excel file that are slowing things down. The tool locates the bottleneck in whole sheets or sets of sheets. Then you will make the requisite adjustments to the file to speed it up.

The main attribute is: It finds bottlenecks in Excel spreadsheets.

Pro tip: Before you use 'Open as App', use 'Bottleneck Detector'. That's how you will save an overly large file from slowing down your mobile device.

Pro tip: With 'Open as App', you can automatically create an app that includes the map sharing link.

XLTools.net Data Cleaning

This is a powerful cleaning tool for Excel. Whenever you import or insert data into a register, you will use it to manage the structure in bulk. It will, among other things, convert cell formats, clean up empty spaces, and alter text events.

The main attribute is: Excel spreadsheets should be cleaned and organized.

Pro tip: This is another Excel add-in that you should use before using 'Open as App' to build an app from a spreadsheet. It will clean up the sheet so your no-code software only shows valuable information.

Handy Map Places & Routes

You can include satellite, road, and street maps in your Excel file using 'HandyMap Places & Routes'. You can insert address and path information directly into a spreadsheet.

The main attribute is: Excel spreadsheets will also have interactive charts.

Duplicate Remover

It is a basic Excel add-in that detects data duplication. It offers you six choices for dealing with each record after they've been found. It makes the task of cleaning up the spreadsheets much easier.

The main attribute is: Locate and exclude redundant material.

Pro tip: This comes in handy when it comes to planning the Excel file for 'Open as App' development.

ASAP Utilities

'ASAP Utilities' is a set of over 300 Excel utilities. They encourage you to perform productive processing, organizing, and other bulk actions. You can save sheets as separate folders, add formulas to specific cells only, and perform a variety of other tasks. The plug-in is accessible in ten different languages.

For Excel, this app has over 300 separate sorting and time-saving tools.

Pro tip: Using 'ASAP Utilities' to arrange the spreadsheet such that it is machine-readable is a brilliant idea. Then you can input it and use 'Open as App' to build an app.

Quandl for Excel

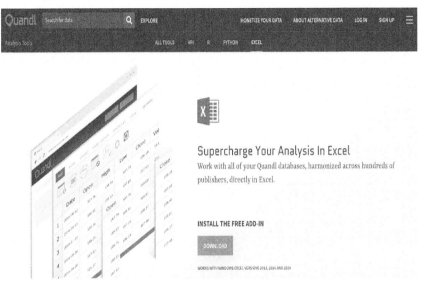

Quandl, a well-known source for financial, economic, and alternate datasets, now has an Excel add-in. With it, you are able to deal with massive databases across the finance industry using Excel's expanded features. It helps you import large amounts of data in order to create reports. You have a lot of options for data discovery in various formats.

The main attribute is: It allows you to quickly insert Quandl datasets into Excel documents.

Pro tip: You should bring the data into Excel with the Quandl add-in, then use the 'Open as App' creator to make an app out of it. It may also be used directly from an API.

Kutools

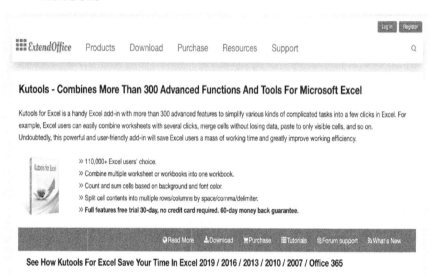

See How Kutools For Excel Save Your Time In Excel 2019 / 2016 / 2013 / 2010 / 2007 / Office 365

In Excel, 'Kutools' adds over 300 additional powerful features. Merging cells with no data loss, mixing worksheets, content translation, and drop-down lists are only a few of the features.

Main feature: In Excel, it simplifies complex activities by reducing them to a few taps.

Pro tip: 'Kutools' makes it simple to build drop-down lists, which are then automatically converted into drop-down menus in your no-code app using 'Open as App'.

QR4Office

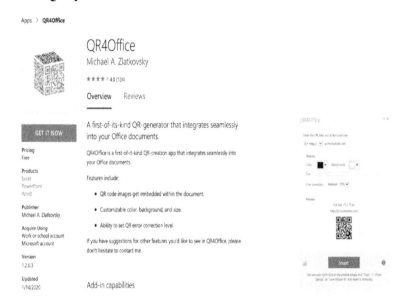

'QR4Office' creates QR codes that can be used with Microsoft Excel. QR codes are a perfect way to easily redirect and lead users to a specific page, and they're helpful for spreadsheets as well as applications. You may change the image's color, context, and scale. After that, you can quickly incorporate it into a spreadsheet.

The main attribute is: Microsoft Office Pro has a QR code creator.

Pro tip: You can save the QR code as a picture and attach it to the Excel file as an icon or a connection. Then, using 'Open as App', incorporate it into the app development process.

Bing Maps

Bing Maps

Microsoft Corporation

★★★☆☆ 3.1 (235)

Overview   Reviews

GET IT NOW

The Bing Maps add-in makes it easy to plot locations and visualize your data through Bing Maps in Excel

Pricing
Free

Products
Excel

Publisher
Microsoft Corporation

Acquire Using
Work or school account
Microsoft account

Version
1.4.0.0

Updated

Bing Maps app for Office helps you use location data from a given column and plot it on a Bing Map. It also provides basic data visualization using your location data.

Plot: Once you launch the app from insert->app, you will see a default map embedded into your Excel spreadsheet. You can select locations from a column and click on the pin icon at the top right to plot them. The header for the column must be selected and the locations should be continuous valued below the header.

Data visualization: You can also select adjacent columns to the right of locations containing data that you want to visualize on the map. If cells from a single adjacent data column is selected, locations are plotted with different sized circles. If multiple data columns are selected, you have the option to either plot them as multiple circles or a pie chart. This can be controlled by clicking on settings icon on the top right.

Microsoft Office has a Bing Maps add-in. It helps you visualize position details in an Excel file using a Bing map. The map settings, such as zooming in and out, can be modified.

The main attribute is: Use an Excel file to plot positions and visualize them on a map.

Chapter 5: Excel Formulas Guide

For beginners to become extremely proficient in financial research, they must first master the simple Excel formulas. Microsoft Excel is widely regarded as the industry norm of data processing applications. In terms of data analysis, financial modeling, and presentation, Microsoft's spreadsheet program is one of the most common among investment bankers and financial analysts. This guide will provide you with an outline of Excel features as well as a selection of the most important ones.

There are two basic ways to perform calculations in Excel:

- Formulas

- Functions

Formulas

A formula in Excel is a user-defined expression that functions on values in a number of cells or a single cell. =A1+A2+A3, for example, finds the total number of the contents of values in cells A1 through A3.

Functions

In Excel, functions are pre-defined formulas. They do away with the time-consuming manual entry of formulas by assigning them human-friendly titles. =SUM(A1:A3), for example. The feature adds up all the values in the cells ranging from A1 to A3.

5.1 Basic Excel Formulas

Since you can now implement and work your chosen formulas, let's look at some essential Excel functions to get you started.

1. SUM

2. AVERAGE

3. COUNT

4. COUNTA

5. IF

6. TRIM

7. MAX

8. MIN

These basic formulas are explained below step by step with examples.

SUM

The SUM function belongs to the Excel Math & Trigonometry functions category. Cells provided as multiple arguments would be summed by the function. It is Excel's most famous and commonly used function.

In MS Excel, SUM allows users to do a simple summation of defined cells. For instance, let's say we're provided the cost of

100 things purchased for a case. The function can be used to calculate the approximate cost of the event.

Formula:

= SUM (num 1, [num 2], [num 3] ......)

The below arguments are used to the SUM function:

- **Number1:** First thing we'd like to sum.

- **Number2:** Second thing we'd like to sum.

- **Number3:** We want to sum up the third object.

The function adds up the values passed in as arguments [up to 255 arguments]. Numbers, ranges, cell references, constants, arrays, and the outputs of other formulas or functions may all be used as arguments.

Example:

Let's say we're provided the following data:

	A	B	C	D
1				
2		SUM Function		
3				
4		Month	Sales	
5		Jan	450	
6		Feb	650	
7		March	900	
8		April	450	
9		May	900	
10		June	890	
11		July	765	
12		August	435	

We'd like to see how much money was earned in the first six months. The following is the formula to use (top right of the image):

| C15 | ▼ | ⋮ | ✕ | ✓ | f_x | =SUM(C5:C10) |

	A	B	C	D
1				
2		**SUM Function**		
3				
4		Month	Sales	
5		Jan	450	
6		Feb	650	
7		March	900	
8		April	450	
9		May	900	
10		June	890	
11		July	765	
12		August	435	
13				
14				
15		Total Sales for first six months	4240	
16				

AVERAGE

The AVERAGE function is a statistical function in Excel. It can return the average value of a series of numbers in Excel. It is a function in Excel that calculates the arithmetic mean of a set of numbers. This guide will show you how to calculate the average in Excel.

This function may be used by a financial analyst to measure the average (mean) of a series of numbers. For example, we may look up a company's 12-month average sales.

Formula:

= AVERAGE (num 1, [num 2], ...)

The following reasons are used by the function:

- **Number1:** This is the very first number in a cell reference, or a range over which the average is desired.

- **Number2:** This can be extra numbers, cell references, or a range over which the average is desired. There are a total of 255 numbers that can be used.

Example

Let's say we're provided the following data:

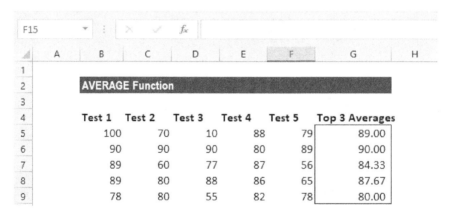

The top three scores according to the above data collection are what we're looking for. The following is the formula to use:

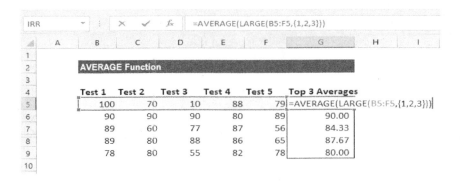

As a consequence, we get the following:

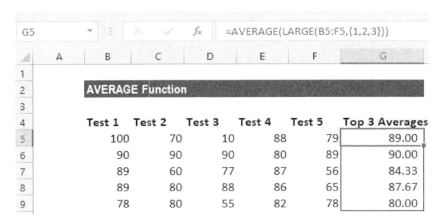

The LARGE function in the above formula obtained the top value from a series of values. Since we used the array constant 1,2,3 into LARGE for the second argument, we got the maximum of three values.

The AVERAGE function was then used to calculate the average of the values. We don't need to use Ctrl + Shift + Enter to enter the formula since the function will manage array effects automatically.

A few details on the AVERAGE function

- Empty cells are ignored by the AVERAGE function.

- Text, logical values, and empty cells are overlooked if a range or cell reference argument includes them. Cells with a value of 0, on the other hand, are used.

- Errors in the function are caused by arguments that are error values or text that can be converted into numbers.

COUNT

The COUNT function is a statistical function of Excel. This function counts the number of cells containing a number and the number of arguments containing numbers. It can also measure the numbers in an array. It first appeared in Excel in the year 2000.

It's helpful as a financial analyst to keep track of the number of cells in a specified range while reviewing results.

Formula:

= COUNT (value 1, value 2....)

- **Value 1:** The first object, cell reference, or range for which we want to count numbers.

- **Value 2:** We may add up to 255 additional objects, cell references, or ranges within those we want to count.

Keep in mind that this feature will only count numbers and will neglect all else.

Consider the following scenarios to better explain how this feature will be used:

Example

Let's have a look at the findings we[A1] get from the details below:

Data	Formula	Result
1/1/17	=COUNT(1-25-2017)	1
25	=COUNT(25)	1
TRUE	=COUNT(TRUE)	0
DIV/0!	=COUNT(#DIV/0!))	0
22.25	=COUNT(22.25)	1
5.25	=COUNT(5.25)	1

As you can see from the example above, the feature overlooked any text or formula errors and instead counted numbers.

The following are the Excel findings we obtained:

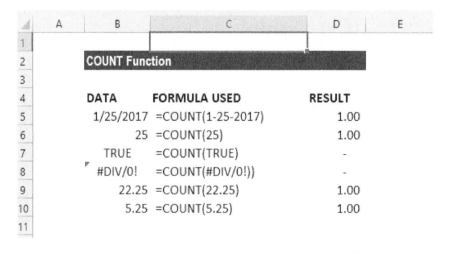

Few Observations

- This feature does not count logical values or errors.

- The feature returned one count per date since Excel stored dates as serial numbers.

An array may be used for this feature. And when we use the COUNT formula =COUNT(B5:B10), we get the following result:

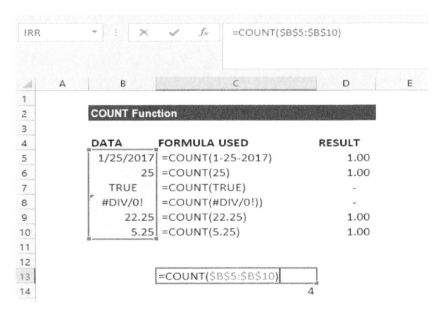

COUNTA

The COUNTA Function belongs to the Excel Statistical Functions category. Inside a given set of values, it can quantify the number of cells that are not blank. This function is also known as the COUNTIF (Not Blank formula) in Excel.

If we want to keep track of how many cells are in a defined range as a financial analyst, we may use the COUNTA function. We frequently need to count cells with values in addition to crunching numbers. The role may be helpful in this situation.

Excel Countif (Not Blank Formula)

= COUNTA (value 1, [value 2], ...)

The following arguments are included in the Excel countif, not blank formula:

- **Value 1:** Value at which we evaluate the function.

- **Value 2:** Additional arguments representing the values to be counted.

Observations on the arguments

- If we use MS Excel 2007 or later, we can join up to 255 value arguments. Only 30 arguments can be handled in previous versions.

- Value arguments can be single values, arrays of values, or cell set references.

Look at the following examples to further explain the COUNTA function.

Example: if not empty

Let's say we're provided the following data:

Data	Formula Used	Result
2/1/2017	=COUNT(2-01-2017)	1.00
35	=COUNT(35)	1.00
TRUE	=COUNT(TRUE)	1.00
#DIV/0!	=COUNT(#DIV/0!))	1.00
22.25	=COUNT(22.25)	1.00
5.25	=COUNT(5.25)	1.00

The COUNTA feature counts text or formula errors, as seen above. COUNTA considers numbers, times, text values, logical values, and errors, unlike the COUNT function, which only considers numbers.

The below are the outcomes:

	A	B	C	D	E
1					
2		COUNTA Function			
3					
4		DATA	FORMULA USED	RESULT	
5		2/1/2017	=COUNT(2-01-2017)	1.00	
6		35	=COUNT(35)	1.00	
7		TRUE	=COUNT(TRUE)	1.00	
8		#DIV/0!	=COUNT(#DIV/0!))	1.00	
9		22.25	=COUNT(22.25)	1.00	
10		5.25	=COUNT(5.25)	1.00	
11					

An array can be counted with the COUNTA function. We can get the result by using the formula =COUNTA (B5:B10), as seen below:

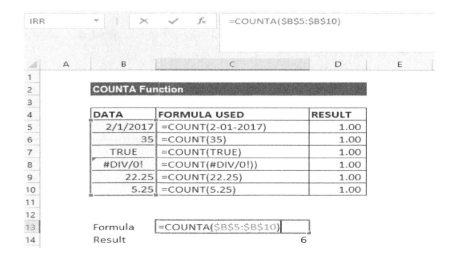

IR | =COUNTA($B$5:$B$10)

DATA	FORMULA USED	RESULT
2/1/2017	=COUNT(2-01-2017)	1.00
35	=COUNT(35)	1.00
TRUE	=COUNT(TRUE)	1.00
#DIV/0!	=COUNT(#DIV/0!))	1.00
22.25	=COUNT(22.25)	1.00
5.25	=COUNT(5.25)	1.00

Formula =COUNTA($B$5:$B$10)
Result 6

IF

The IF Statement in Excel evaluates a condition and returns one value for a TRUE outcome and another value for a FALSE outcome. If revenue totals more than $5,000, for example, select "Yes" for Bonus; otherwise, select "No" for Bonus. We may use the IF function to determine a single function or several IF functions in a single formula. In Excel, nested IF statements are a set of multiple statements.

The IF function is often utilized by financial analysts to interpret and examine data by analyzing particular situations.

Text, values, and perhaps even errors may all be evaluated with this function. It's not all about comparing two things and returning a single answer. Depending on our parameters, we may also use mathematical variables and perform additional calculations. To perform multiple comparisons, we can nest multi IF functions together.

Formula

=IF (logical test, value if true, value if false)

The following reasons are used by the function:

- **Logical test:** Condition to be checked and assessed as TRUE or FALSE is defined by the logical test (required argument).

- **Value if true:** If the logical test evaluates to TRUE, the value if true (optional argument) will be returned.

- **Value if false:** If the logical test evaluates to FALSE, the value if false (optional argument) will be returned.

The below logical operators can be used with the IF feature to construct a test:

= this indicates equal to

> this indicates greater than

>= this indicates greater than or equal to

< this indicates less than

<= this indicates less than or equal to

<> this indicates not equal to

Example

Let's say we want to run a quick examination. We want to see whether cell C2's value is greater than or equivalent to cell D2's value. If the assertion is true, we want to show "Yes it is," and if the argument is false, we want to display "No, it isn't."

In the basic illustration below, you will see how the Excel IF argument functions.

When true, the following is the outcome:

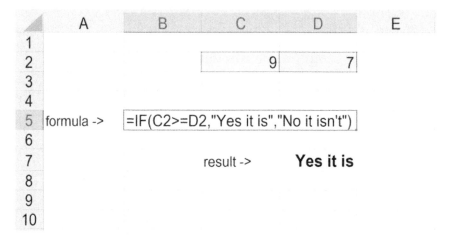

When false, the following is the outcome:

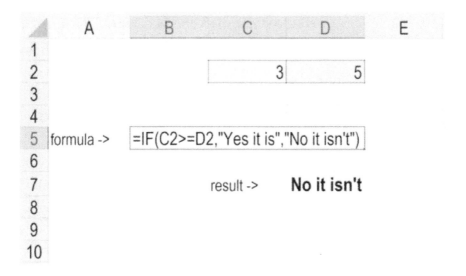

	A	B	C	D	E
1					
2			3	5	
3					
4					
5	formula ->	=IF(C2>=D2,"Yes it is","No it isn't")			
6					
7			result ->	No it isn't	
8					
9					
10					

Trim

The TRIM feature is part of the Excel Text functions category. TRIM helps clean the cells in the worksheet by removing extra spaces in data.

The TRIM feature may be useful in financial analysis for eliminating uneven spacing from data that is imported via other applications.

Formula

=TRIM (text)

- **Text:** This is the text from which we want to delete spaces (required argument).

A couple of notes on the TRIM Function:

- Extra spaces in the text can be removed with TRIM. As a result, only single spaces can be left between words, with no space characters at the beginning or end of the text.

- It comes in handy when you need to clean up text from other apps or environments.

- The ASCII space character (32) is the only character that TRIM removes from the text.

- A non-breaking space character (160) is often used in Unicode text and exists as a HTML object in web pages. With TRIM, it will not be replaced.

In Excel, the built-in function TRIM may be used as a worksheet function. Find the following explanations to better understand the function's applications:

Example

Let's say we're sent the following data from an outside source:

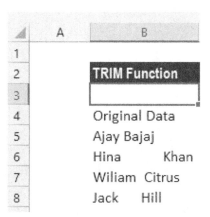

We'll use the following feature to trim the spaces:

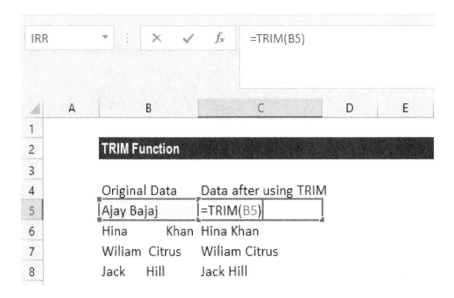

The below are the outcomes:

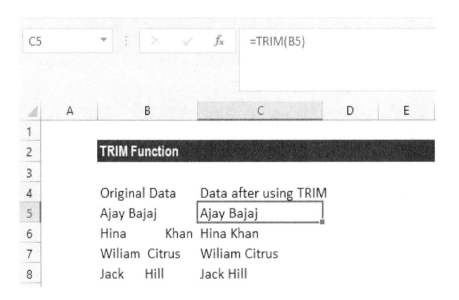

Max Function

The MAX Function belongs to the Excel Statistical Functions category. The largest value in a specified list of arguments will be returned by MAX. It will return the maximum value from a series of numeric values. The MAX function counts numbers but ignores blank cells, the logical values, text, TRUE & FALSE, and text values, unlike the MAXA function.

MAX may be used in financial reporting to calculate the maximum score, quickest period, revenue amount, or highest expense, and so on.

Formula

=MAX (num 1, [num 2], ...)

Num 1 & Num 2 are the function's arguments, with Number1 being necessary and the remaining values being optional.

The MAX function in Excel 2007 & later versions will take up to 250 additional number arguments. Excel 2003 & earlier versions, on the other hand, will only consider up to 30 number arguments.

Constants, cell references, and ranges may both be used as arguments. The MAX function can neglect null cells, text, and logical values present within the supplied cell range if an argument is delivered to the function as a guide to a cell or an array of cells. However, the equation will contain conceptual values & text representation of numbers that are supplied directly to the function.

The MAX function is a worksheet function that can be used in a formula in a worksheet cell. Find the following examples to better explain the function's applications:

Example

Let's see what the highest marks are based on the following information:

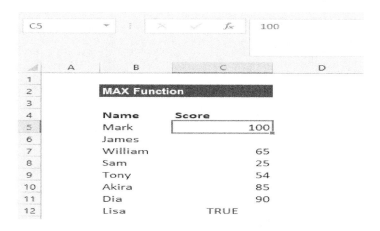

The formula was as follows:

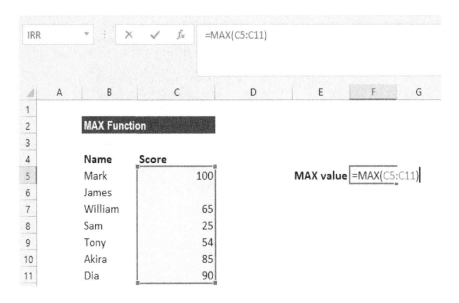

The empty value was ignored by the MAX feature, which returned 100 as a result.

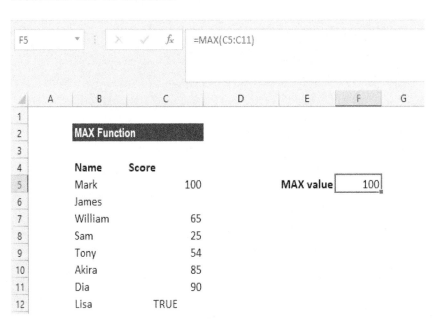

MAX, as previously said, ignores empty values. If we have a logical meaning, in this case, the function will overlook it and return the same answer, as seen below:

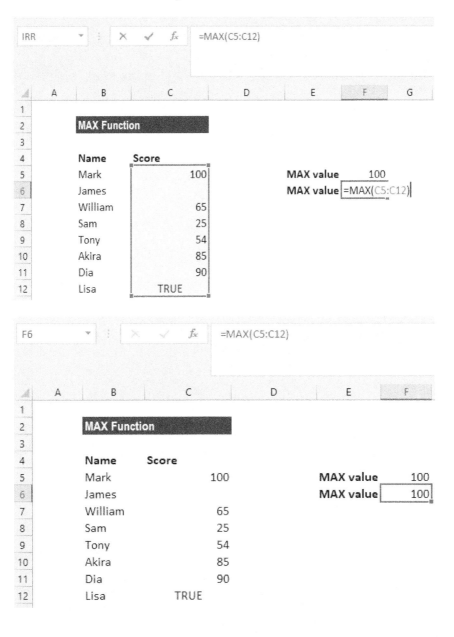

Points to keep in mind while using the MAX Function

- #VALUE! If all the values passed directly to the MAX function are non-numeric, an error would occur.

- MAX returns 0 if arguments do not contain any numbers.

- MAXA evaluates TRUE and FALSE values as 1 and 0, respectively, while MAX evaluates them as 1 and 0[A2]. As a result, we must use the MAXA feature if we choose to use conceptual values.

Min Function

The MIN function is part of the Excel Statistical functions category. The minimum value in a specified list of arguments is returned by MIN. It will return the lower value from a series of numeric values. The MIN algorithm, unlike the MINA function, disregards text, numbers, and logical values TRUE & FALSE, as well as text values.

The MIN method can be used to calculate debt schedules and depreciation schedules in financial modeling.

Formula

=MIN (number1, [number2], ...)

The MIN function in MS Excel 2007 and later versions will take up to 255 number arguments. Excel 2003 and older models, on the other hand, will only consider up to 30 number arguments.

Constants, cell references, and ranges may both be used as arguments. The MIN function will neglect null cells and text or logical values found within the supplied cell set if an argument is delivered to the function as a guide to a cell or an array of cells. However, the equation will contain conceptual values & text representations of numbers that are supplied directly to the function.

The MIN function is a worksheet function that can be used in a formula in a worksheet cell. The following example better explains the function's applications.

Example

Let's see what the lowest score is based on the following information:

	A	B	C
1			
2		MIN Function	
3			
4		Name	Score
5		Mark	100
6		James	
7		William	65
8		Sam	25
9		Tony	54
10		Akira	85
11		Dia	90
12		Lisa	TRUE

The formula was as follows:

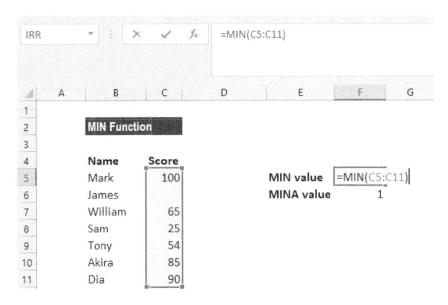

The empty value was overlooked by the MIN function, which resulted in a value of 25.

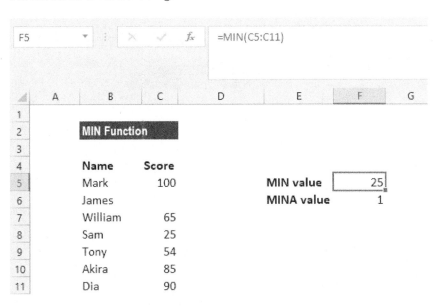

MIN, as previously said, ignores empty values. If we have a logical meaning, in this case, the function will overlook it and return the same outcome, but MINA will take it into account, as seen below:

F7	▾ : × ✓ fx	=MIN(C5:C12)

◢	A	B	C	D	E	F	G
1							
2		MIN Function					
3							
4		Name	Score				
5		Mark	100		MIN value	25	
6		James			MINA value	1	
7		William	65		MIN value	25	
8		Sam	25				
9		Tony	54				
10		Akira	85				
11		Dia	90				
12		Lisa	TRUE				

Few points to keep in mind while using the MIN Feature.

- #Value! If all the values delivered straight to the MIN function are non-numeric, an error will occur.

- The main distinction between MIN & MINA is that MINA measures TRUE & FALSE values as 1 and 0, respectively, whereas MIN evaluates them as 0. As a result, we could use the MINA function to use conceptual values.

5.2 Advanced Excel Formulas: Introduction

Before jumping to the advanced Excel Formulas, let's take a moment to understand what is advanced excel.

Advanced Excel

Advanced Excel is a highly sought-after talent. As of January 2020, a fast search on LinkedIn revealed over 68k positions worldwide requiring specialized Excel skills.

Linked In's specialized Excel quest yielded 68,292 data.

The occupations that were mentioned on LinkedIn were mostly for financial positions, such as Financial Analyst or Financial Planning Manager, though the positions were spread around different regions and industries.

The following is a compilation of positions that need specialized Excel skills.

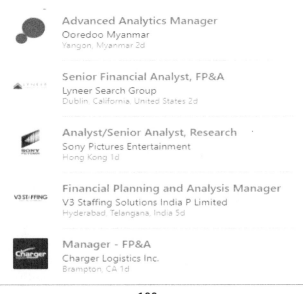

Advanced Analytics Manager
Ooredoo Myanmar
Yangon, Myanmar 2d

Senior Financial Analyst, FP&A
Lyneer Search Group
Dublin, California, United States 2d

Analyst/Senior Analyst, Research
Sony Pictures Entertainment
Hong Kong 1d

Financial Planning and Analysis Manager
V3 Staffing Solutions India P Limited
Hyderabad, Telangana, India 5d

Manager - FP&A
Charger Logistics Inc.
Brampton, CA 1d

However, there is no consensus about what advanced Excel entails.

Advanced Excel is described as "highly skilled with Microsoft Office and especially Excel" in one job description (i.e., lookups, pivot tables, advanced formulas).

In another case, it necessitated a broader capability set.

Advanced Excel functions are needed for the majority of job descriptions. These workers didn't break down the different kinds of Excel abilities that make up an advanced knowledge of the program.

The Microsoft Office Specialist credential tests are the first place to look if you want to learn more about how Microsoft describes advanced Excel.

What does it mean to be an Excel Associate?

Microsoft's official collection of Excel Associate capabilities contains the following:

1. Workbooks and Worksheets should be managed.

2. Organize data into ranges and cells.

3. Formulas and tasks are used to carry out activities.

4. Organize charts.

5. Tables and data can be controlled.

At the Associate stage, the aim will not be to be able to create complicated spreadsheets. Instead, the target must be able to interact with models created by more experienced Excel users.

At this step, the following functions are referenced by name:

1. LEFT()[A3] and LOWER() are text functions ().

2. MAX() and SUM() are two basic calculation features ().

3. The IF() method may be used to create simple conditional logic.

An Excel associate might be asked to function on a sheet provided by a more experienced person. They could even make any changes to a cover. They will, though, struggle to create a spreadsheet without assistance.

Exams with Office Specialists

According to the Microsoft certification pages, there are currently five Microsoft Excel exams online.

Exams for Office specialists are mentioned below.

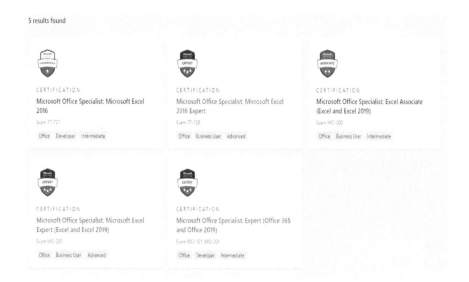

CERTIFICATION
Microsoft Office Specialist: Microsoft Excel 2016
Exam 77-727
Office Developer Intermediate

CERTIFICATION
Microsoft Office Specialist: Microsoft Excel 2016 Expert
Exam 77-728
Office Business User Advanced

CERTIFICATION
Microsoft Office Specialist: Excel Associate (Excel and Excel 2019)
Exam MO-200
Office Business User Intermediate

CERTIFICATION
Microsoft Office Specialist: Microsoft Excel Expert (Excel and Excel 2019)
Exam MO-201
Office Business User Advanced

CERTIFICATION
Microsoft Office Specialist: Expert (Office 365 and Office 2019)
Exam MO-101 MO-201
Office Developer Intermediate

Two of the tests are for Excel 2016 rather than Excel 2019 / 365, although they are being phased out in favor of more recent exams. The highly advanced test is a mixture of Word through Excel, and it does not specify what is assessed in this exam.

In fact, there are two exams:

1. Excel Associate

2. Microsoft Excel Expert is a Microsoft Office Specialist

What does it mean to be an Excel expert?

The qualifications offered by Microsoft for the Excel Expert test are adequate enough to fulfil the specifications of the majority of jobs that demand specialized Excel skills.

1. Options and configurations for the workbook may be controlled.

2. Data management and formatting.

3. Make complex calculations and macros.

4. Manage complex graphs and tables.

The following are examples of named functions at this stage: -

1. INDEX(), VLOOKUP(), and MATCH()

2. PMT is one of the most basic financial features ().

3. SUMIFS and other conditional column formulas ().

Pivot tables, as well as capturing and copying simple macros, are all covered at this stage. A person has progressed from being able to deal in spreadsheets to be able to create spreadsheets from a variety of data sources.

What are advanced Excel principles that are missing as an Excel guru?

While the Excel Expert test can cover anything you need to know to produce a spreadsheet from a data source, it leaves out a lot of valuable details for current Excel processes.

More advanced elements that are not discussed include:

1. Mathematical, financial, and statistical formulas.

2. VBA programming.

3. PowerPivot (both M and DAX).

Additional Formulas

Function Library

The Excel Expert exam gives you a clear rundown of some of the most important data processing features like VLOOKUP() and conditional formulas like SUMIFS ().

Also, at the associate stage, it offers a clear introduction to text functions!

It does not, however, use math functions like RAND and instead gives a simple introduction to financial functions (the PMT() function) ().

The SUBSTITUTE() and TRIM() functions are noteworthy omissions in the text manipulation portion. If Power Query isn't accessible, these functions ensure the data is imported correctly.

Pivot Point (M and DAX)

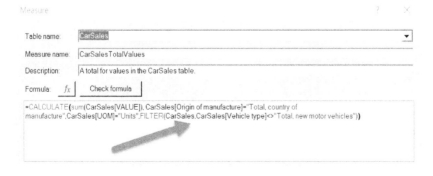

Microsoft does not actually sell any certifications or tests for the M or DAX programming languages. This is a shame, for these are essential features in Modern Excel.

While these methods provide a graphical GUI, it is advised that you use some supplementary resources to get started with programming languages!

Programming in Visual Basic for Applications (VBA)

Given Microsoft's emphasis on other technologies (such as Automate or Power Query), learning VBA might not be useful. This opinion was presented by a 2019 StackOverflow poll, which found that VBA was the most feared programming language among developers.

This isn't to suggest that VBA isn't a valuable programming tool. Other programming languages, on the other hand, could be more useful.

There is no simple example of what an experienced Excel consumer is capable of. Microsoft's Expert description suits the demands of the work sector, but it leaves out certain important terms.

Advanced Excel consumers must be familiar with computer principles that did not apply ten years prior.

Users with expertise not included by the Excel Expert credential would be the most valuable to businesses in the coming years.

5.3 Advanced Excel Formulas

Many financial analyst' spends much more time in Excel than he or she would like to admit. We've gathered the most relevant and sophisticated Excel formulas that any world-class financial analyst should recognize based on years of experience.

1. INDEX MATCH

2. IF, jointly with AND / OR

3. OFFSET, jointly with SUM or AVERAGE

4. CHOOSE

5. XIRR and XNPV

6. COUNTIF and SUMIF

7. IPMT and PMT

8. TRIM and LEN

9. CONCATENATE

10. CELL, MID, RIGHT, and LEFT functions

These formulas are explained below with examples.

INDEX MATCH

This is a more advanced version of the VLOOKUP / HLOOKUP formulas (which have a number of flaws and limitations). INDEX MATCH is a versatile Excel formula combination that can help you improve your financial analysis & modeling.

INDEX is a table function that returns the value of a cell depending on the column & row number.

The place of a cell in a column OR row is returned by the MATCH function.

Here's an example of combining the INDEX & MATCH formulas. We look up and return a person's height based on their name in this case. We should adjust both the name and the height in the calculation since they are both variables.

	A	B	C	D	E	F	G
1							
2			1	2	3		
3		1	Name	Height	Weight		
4		2	Sally	6.2	185		
5		3	Tom	5.9	170		
6		4	Kevin	5.8	175		
7		5	Amanda	5.5	145		
8		6	Carl	6.1	210		
9		7	Ned	6.0	180		
10							
11							
12			=INDEX(C3:E9,MATCH(B13,C3:C9,0),MATCH(B14,C3:E3,0))				
13		Kevin					
14		Height					

IF jointly with AND / OR

Anyone who has spent a significant amount of time working with different forms of financial principles understands how difficult nested IF formulas can be. Combining the IF feature with the AND or OR function will keep formulas simpler to audit and understand for other users. You will see how we combined the individual functions to construct a more advanced formula in the illustration below.

	A	B	C	D	E	F	G
1							
2		Data Cell	150				
3							
4		Condition 1	100	>=			
5		Condition 2	999	<=			
6		Result if true	100				
7		Result if fales	0				
8							
9		Live Formula	=IF(AND(C2>=C4,C2<=C5),C6,C7)				
10							
11							

OFFSET jointly with SUM or AVERAGE

= SUM (B4: OFFSET (B4,0, E2-1))

The OFFSET feature is not very sophisticated on its own, but when combined with other functions like SUM or AVERAGE, we can build a very complex formula. Consider the following scenario: you want to build a complex feature that can sum a variable number of cells. You can only do a static calculation using the normal SUM formula, but by adding OFFSET, you can shift the cell reference around.

The OFFSET formula is used to replace the SUM function's finishing reference cell. This is what makes the formula complex, and you can tell Excel how many sequential cells you want to sum up in the cell referenced as E2.

This much more sophisticated formula is shown in the screenshot below.

	A	B	C	D	E	F	G	H
1								
2		Sum this many numbers:			3			
3								
4		5	8	2	9	6	4	
5								
6		Solution						
7				=SUM(B4:OFFSET(B4,0,E2-1))			Formula	
8					15		Value	
9								
10								
11								

The SUM formula begins in cell B4, but it finishes with a variable, which is the OFFSET formula, which begins in cell B4 and continues by the value in E2 ("3"), minus one. This shifts the sum formula's end over two cells, summing three years of details (including the starting point). The number of cells B4:D4 is 15, as seen in cell F7; that is what the offset & sum formula provides us.

CHOOSE

The CHOOSE feature is ideal for financial simulation scenario study. It encourages you to choose from a set of choices and has the ability to return the "choice" you've made. Assume you have three separate sales growth assumptions for next year: 5%, 12%, and 18%. If you informed Excel, you want option #2, you will get a 12% return using the CHOOSE formula.

▲	A	B	C	D	E	F	G
1							
2							
3			Option 1	5%			
4			Option 2	12%			
5			Option 3	18%			
6							
7		Selection ->	2	=CHOOSE(C7,D3,D4,D5)			
8							
9							
10							
11							

XIRR and XNPV

Formula = XNPV (cash flows, discount rate, dates)

These formulas can come in handy if you work in investment management, market research, financial analysis & planning (FA & P), or another field of corporate finance that includes discounting cash flows.

Simply put, XIRR and XNPV enables you to assign specific dates to each discounted cash flow. The simple IRR and NPV formulas in Excel have the flaw in assuming that the time intervals between cash flows are equivalent. As an analyst, you will see conditions where cash balances are not perfectly aligned on a regular basis, and this formula is how you solve it.

◢	A	B	C	D	E	F	G	H	I
1									
2									
3		Dates		5/18/2018	12/31/2018	9/12/2019	12/25/2019	5/8/2020	12/31/2020
4									
5		Cash Flows		1,000	1,000	1,000	1,000	1,000	1,000
6									
7		Discount Rate		10.0%					
8									
9		XNPV	=XNPV(D7,D5:I5,D3:I3)	Formula					
10				5,289	Value				
11									

COUNTIF and SUMIF

Conditional functions are used effectively in these advanced formulas. All cells that fulfil certain criteria are included in SUMIF, and all cells that fulfil the certain criteria are counted in COUNTIF. For example, suppose you want to figure out how many bottles of champagne you want for a client event by counting all cells that are greater or equivalent to 21 (the minimum drink age in the United States). As seen in the image below, COUNTIF may be used as an advanced approach.

◢	A	B	C	D	E	F	G	H
1								
2								
3								
4				Age				
5				19				
6				26				
7				20				
8				19				
9				29				
10				31				
11				21				
12				25				
13								
14				=COUNTIF(D5:D12,">=21")				
15								

IPMT and PMT

You will need to know these two formulas if you operate in commercial banking, real estate, FP&A, or another financial analyst job that deals with debt schedules.

The PMT formula calculates the worth of making equivalent payments over the course of a loan's existence. You should use that in combination with IPMT (which shows you how much interest you will pay for the same kind of loan).

Here's how to use the PMT feature to calculate the monthly mortgage payment on a $1 million loan with a 5% interest rate over 30 years.

	A	B	C	D	E
1					
2					
3		Rate	5.0%		
4		# Periods	30		
5		Loan Value	1,000,000		
6					
7		PMT	=PMT(C3,C4,C5,1) Formula		
8		PMT	61,954 Value		
9		Monthly PMT	5,163		
10					

TRIM and LEN

Formulas =TRIM (text) and = LEN (text)

The formulas mentioned above are a little less popular, but they are definitely sophisticated. Financial analysts who need to organize and manipulate vast volumes of data may benefit from them. Unfortunately, the data we receive is not necessarily well-organized, and problems such as extra spaces at the start or end of cells will arise.

The LEN formula returns the number of characters in a specified text string, which is helpful when you need to count how many characters are in a text.

You will see how the formula of TRIM cleans up the Excel data in the illustration below.

	A	B	C	D	E	F	G
1							
2							
3		No Extra spaces					
4		Example of extra spaces			=TRIM(B4)		
5					⇩		
6							
7		Example of extra spaces			Example of extra spaces		
8							
9							
10							

CONCATENATE

Formula =A1&" more text"

Concatenate isn't even a function in itself; it's just a creative way of gathering data from multiple cells together and creating worksheets more complex. For financial analysts working with financial simulation, this is a really useful instrument.

In the illustration below, the text "New York" plus "is combined with "NY" to form "New York, NY." This enables you to build complex worksheet headers and labels. Instead of upgrading cell B8, you can upgrade cells B2 & D2 separately. This is a great attribute to have while dealing with a huge data collection.

	A	B	C	D	E	F
1						
2		New York		NY		
3						
4						
5		=B2&", "&D2				
6		⇩				
7						
8		New York, NY				
9						
10						
11						

CELL, MID, RIGHT, and LEFT functions

These advanced Excel features may be combined to produce certain complicated and advanced formulas. The CELL feature may return a range of data about a cell's contents (such as its row, column, name, location, and more). The LEFT function returns the text from the cell's beginning (left to right), the MID function returns the text from any cell's start point (left to right), and the RIGHT function returns the text from the cell's end (right to the left).

The three formulations are shown in the diagram below.

	A	B	C	D	E	F
1						
2						
3		New York, NY		=LEFT(B3,3)	⇨	New
4						
5				=MID(B3,5,4)	⇨	York
6						
7				=RIGHT(B3,2)	⇨	NY
8						
9						
10						
11						

Chapter 6: Excel advanced features and functions

One of the most popular methods for calculating, analyzing, and visualizing data and details is with the use of Microsoft Office Excel. It uses columns and rows, as well as some fun MS Excel features, to help people coordinate and process info.

6.1 Vlookup

This feature aids in finding meaning in a table. It returns a value that corresponds to the input. In other terms, it looks for the specified value and returns a value from another column that matches it.

The attribute to check for is the lookup value in the above syntax. It may be an email, a date, or a phone number. Two or more data columns make up a table array. The column number in the table array from which the value in the comparable row should be retrieved is col index num.

6.2 Mixed or Combination Type Charts

One of MS Excel's most useful functions is the mixed or combination chart. In a single chart, it blends and shows information from two or more chart varieties.

Follow these measures to construct a combination chart:

- **Select the range A1: C13.**

	A	B	C	D
1	Month	Rainy Days	Profit	
2	Jan	12	$3,574	
3	Feb	11	$4,708	
4	Mar	10	$5,332	
5	Apr	9	$6,693	
6	May	8	$8,843	
7	Jun	6	$12,347	
8	Jul	4	$15,180	
9	Aug	6	$11,198	
10	Sep	7	$9,739	
11	Oct	8	$9,846	
12	Nov	10	$6,620	
13	Dec	11	$5,085	
14				

• Now, in the Charts group of the Insert tab, press the Combo icon and then generate a custom combo chart.

• A dialogue box to attach a chart will open. Select the clustered column as the chart style for the rainy days series. After that, pick the line chart form for the profit series. The profit series can now be plotted on the secondary axis.

- **After that, click OK, and it will show the output.**

One of the most amazing Microsoft Excel advanced features and functionality is a mixed or combination chart.

6.3 Pie Chart

One of the most useful functions of Microsoft Excel is the pie chart. It's used to show how each value contributes to the overall pie diagram. It only uses one data series at a time.

Follow the steps provided below to create a pie chart:

- **Select the range A1: D2.**

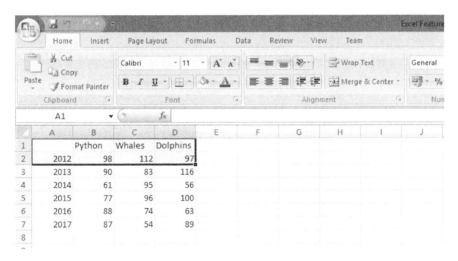

- **Now, click the Pie icon in the Charts group on the Insert page, then click Pie.**

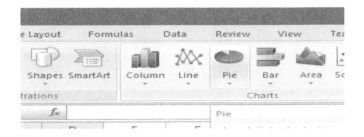

The result will be shown to you in the form of a pie chart.

6.4 Data Validation

One of Excel's most powerful features is data validation. It ensures that user's type-specific values into a cell.

6.5 Remove Duplicates

For people who act as data analysts or who work with data on a daily basis, removing duplicates is the most powerful MS Excel function. This example demonstrates how to delete duplicates from an Excel spreadsheet. Remove Duplicates can be found on the Data tab, in the Data Tools group, by clicking every single cell within the data set.

The dialogue box that follows will appear. Now, review all of the checkboxes and press OK.

Except for the first identical row, MS Excel can eliminate all identical rows (blue).

You can try out these free plugins to erase duplicates, sort, and clean lines in Google Docs / Google Sheets: Lines Sorter and Cleaner plugin for Google Sheets, and Lines Sorter and Cleaner plugin for Google Docs.

6.6 IF ERROR Function

IFERROR is one of the coolest specialized Excel formulas and features if you work in the area of data processing. When a method produces an error, it returns a result, and when no error is detected, it returns a normal result. IFERROR is a basic error management system that avoids the use of nested IF statements.

6.7 Conditional Formatting

This allows you to adjust the format of a cell based on its text, a number of cells, or another cell or cells in the worksheet or a spreadsheet. It also helps users to notice relevant trends in data and highlight mistakes. Cell formatting and basic fonts, such as font color, number size, cell boundaries, and other font attributes, may be applied using conditional formats. There are also various conditional formats that enable data visualization by the use of color scales, icon sets, or data bars.

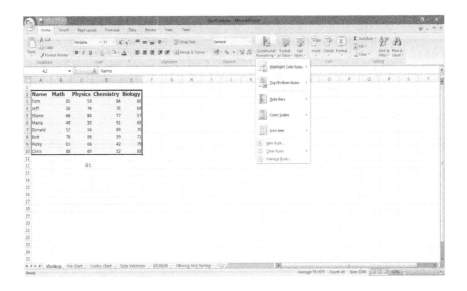

6.8 DB Function

The DB role in Microsoft Excel is a financial function. It helps users to measure an asset's depreciation. For each cycle of the asset's lifespan, the fixed-declining balance form is used.

6.9 MINVERSE

The MINVERSE function in Microsoft Excel returns the opposite matrix of a given matrix. This function belongs to the Math/Trig Function category.

6.10 Visualization of Data

Data and data visualization are one of Microsoft Excel's most important features. Excel's Sparkline mode is fantastic. It's also used as a visualization method for MS Excel, and it allows users to see the general pattern within a series of values in great detail. Sparklines, in a nutshell, are mini-graphs contained within cells. Sparklines are shown in the following case.

Salesman	Jan'15	Feb'15	Mar'15	Apr'15	May'15	Jun'15
John	41,234	42,220	42,486	42,944	43,081	43,603
Peter	44,730	43,091	44,976	47,406	50,802	49,996
Brooke	51,402	50,798	50,481	50,238	49,818	49,499
Mary	51,966	48,518	47,437	50,971	51,242	54,388

6.11 MKDIR

Is a function of MS Excel, and it is the most underappreciated one of all. It's categorized as a File/Directory Feature. MKDIR is a VBA feature that can be used to create new directories. It's possible to use it in macro code written in the Microsoft Visual Basic Editor.

6.12 Complex Function

The COMPLEX function combines real and imaginary coefficients to produce a complex number like, x + yi or x + yj.

6.13 IF and OR function

The IF and OR functions in Excel are helpful if you wish to obtain a binary answer. In other words, whether you want to get a False or True, or Fail or Pass answer, you can use the IF or OR feature. Our formula begins with an IF function, which is then followed by the OR function. Have a look at the screenshot below.

	TRUE		▼	X ✓	*fx*	=IF(OR(B2>=35,C2>=35),"Pass","Fail")	

	A	B	C	D	E	F	G
1	Students	Subject 1	Subject 2				
2	A	45	52	=IF(OR(B2>=35,C2>=35),"Pass","Fail")			
3	B	50	49				
4	C	28	64				
5	D	76	25				
6	E	30	32				
7	F	58	45				
8	G	32	40				
9	H	64	79				

The Pass or Fail outcome will now appear when you click enter and drag the fill handle. Have a look at the screenshot below.

	D2		▼		*fx*	=IF(OR(B2>=35,C2>=35),"Pass","Fail")	

	A	B	C	D	E	F	G
1	Students	Subject 1	Subject 2				
2	A	45	52	Pass			
3	B	50	49	Pass			
4	C	28	64	Pass			
5	D	76	25	Pass			
6	E	30	32	Fail			
7	F	58	45	Pass			
8	G	32	40	Pass			
9	H	64	79	Pass			
10							

6.14 Transpose

Users may use the TRANSPOSE feature to create a transposed set of cells. When a vertical range is entered as an input, it returns a horizontal range of cells. Where a horizontal range of cells is entered as an input, a vertical range of cells is returned. It's part of Microsoft Excel's Lookup/Reference Feature.

6.15 Hyperlink

You may build a shortcut to a file or a website address using Excel's HYPERLINK feature. To make a hyperlink, go to the Insert tab and choose Hyperlink from the Links group.

A dialogue box titled "Insert Hyperlink" will appear. Pick a file to build a connection to an Excel file that has already been developed.

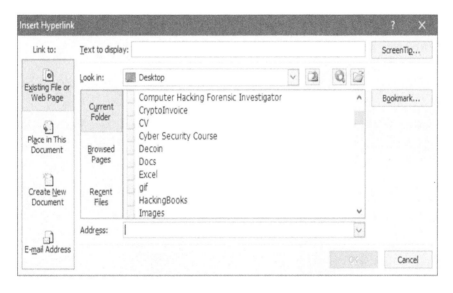

Now, type the text to display and press OK to create a link to a web page. We entered google.com as the text to view, and the effect is seen in the picture below.

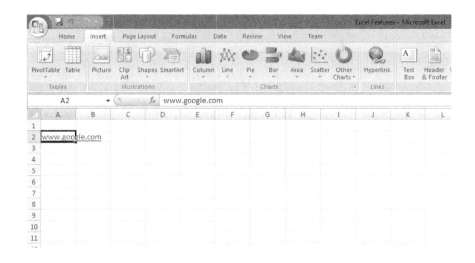

6.16 INDIRECT

Based on the string definition of a cell, this feature returns a reference to that cell. It's part of MS Excel's Lookup/Reference Function. It returns the value of the referenced cell.

6.17 CONCATENATE

CONCATENATE function enables the individuals to join two or more strings together.

THE FOLLOWING FIGURE IS SHOWING US THE USE OF THE CONCATENATE FUNCTION:

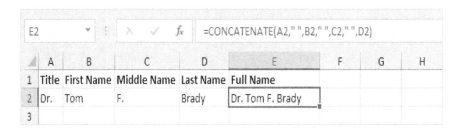

6.18 FORMAT

The FORMAT method takes a string as a variable and returns a formatted string. It's part of Microsoft Excel's String/Text Feature.

LET'S LOOK AT SOME EXCEL FORMAT FUNCTION EXAMPLES:

	E	F	G	H
	G23		fx	
1				
2		Example	25-Oct-16	
3			25Oct2016	=TEXT($G$2,"DDMMMYYYY")
4			25Oct16	=TEXT($G$2,"DDMMMYY")
5			Oct 25, 2016	=TEXT($G$2,"MMM DD, YYYY")
6			Tuesday	=TEXT($G$2,"DDDD")
7		DATE	Tuesday, 25Oct2016	=TEXT($G$2,"DDDD, DDMMMYYYY")
8			Tuesday, Oct 25, 2016	=TEXT($G$2,"DDDD, MMM DD, YYYY")
9			10/25/2016	=TEXT($G$2,"MM/DD/YYYY")
10			10/25	=TEXT($G$2,"MM/DD")
11			2016-10-25	=TEXT($G$2,"YYYY-MM-DD")
12		Example	10:28	
13			10:28 AM	=TEXT($G$12,"H:MM AM/PM")
14		TIME	10:28:00 AM	=TEXT($G$12,"H:MM:SS AM/PM")
15			10:53:30 PM	=TEXT(NOW(),"H:MM:SS AM/PM")
16		Example	2016/10/25 15:28	
17			Oct 25, 2016 3:28:00 PM	=TEXT($G$16,"MMM DD, YYYY H:MM:SS AM/PM")
18		DATE TIME	2016-10-25 3:28 PM	=TEXT($G$16,"YYYY-MM-DD H:MM AM/PM")
19			2016-10-25 15:28	=TEXT($G$16,"YYYY-MM-DD H:MM")

Figure 2.2

6.19 Paste Special

One of Excel's most useful functionality's is Paste Special. When content is pasted from the clipboard, it allows the user to monitor how it is viewed. The illustration below demonstrates how to use Paste special.

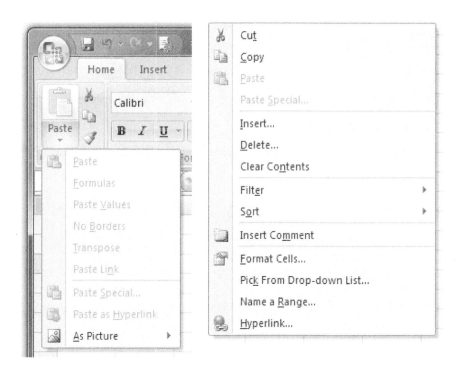

6.20 ROUND Function

This is one of the most valuable tools in Microsoft Excel. The round function is used to take an integer of several decimals and round it to the required number of decimals.

The Round feature is shown in the following picture. In column D, we have split labor into total expenses. The considerable number after the decimal would be demonstrated if we simply use the formula B2/C2.

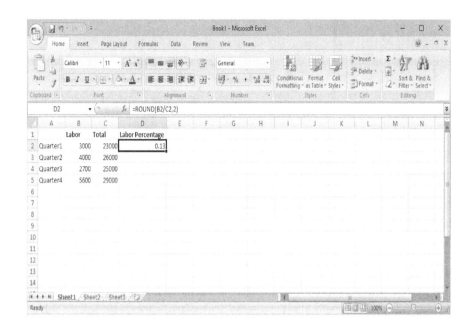

6.21 TRIM

The TRIM feature is helpful if you want to delete extra spaces from a spreadsheet. The trim feature removes all of the cell's unused trailing and leading spaces.

The TRIM feature is shown in the diagram above. The unused spaces in column A have been removed, and the effect is seen in column C.

6.22 PROPER

Any of the entered phrases are converted into a professional-looking style or sentence case using the PROPER function. It's a text function that capitalizes each term in a sentence.

The PROPER function is shown in the following picture.

It doesn't matter what the spectrum is. The function is a string function that converts the text into the correct sentence case.

If users are working with text spreadsheets when migrating information, the PROPER function is critical. Converting text into correct sentence form is easy to enforce and use.

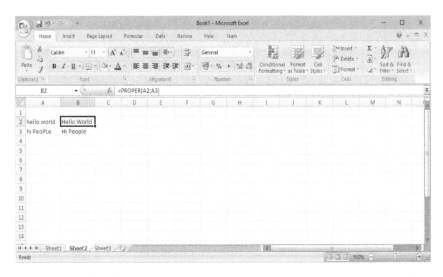

6.23 CHOOSE function

In commercial modeling, the CHOOSE function is ideal for overview study. It allows users to choose from a set of options and then reacts to the chosen option. For, e.g., there are three distinct sales growth projections for the coming year: 5%, 12%, and 18%. If users know Excel wants options, they will return 12% using the CHOOSE algorithm. The outcome is seen in the picture below.

	A	B	C	D	E	F	G
1							
2							
3			Option 1	5%			
4			Option 2	12%			
5			Option 3	18%			
6							
7		Selection ->	2	=CHOOSE(C7,D3,D4,D5)			
8							
9							
10							
11							

6.24 NOW function

The NOW function is straightforward. It's a simple feature that tells users what time it is and what day it is. Users may format it to display the date and time, or only the date by using this feature.

The usage of the NOW() function is shown in the following picture. After you enter the formula =NOW() in cell B3, cell B3 displays the current date on your device.

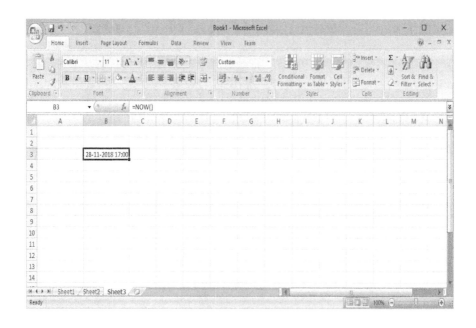

6.25 Named Ranges

This is one of Excel's most useful advanced functions. If there are a lot of numbers, this function will help users name ranges so they can refer to them in advanced Excel formulas without having to press and select long ranges. Take these measures to assign the ranges titles:

- On the ribbon, choose the Formulas menu option.

- In the next section, choose the Create from Selection icon.

- In the third stage, select the ranges to name.

The use of Named Ranges is shown in the following illustration.

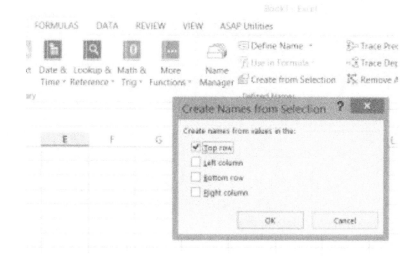

6.26 Quick Feature

This is one of the most sophisticated Excel software resources available. Without using any formulas, this function provides composite statistics such as Count, Average, Numerical Count, Min, Max, and Amount for data from a selected set.

Right-click on the toolbar and choose the desired figure to show these findings in the bottom toolbar. This function is demonstrated in the following picture. If users need to aggregate numbers quickly, the quick feature comes in handy.

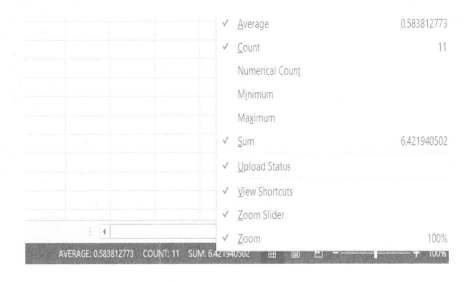

6.27 New Shortcut Menu

On the top menu, there are typically three shortcuts. Undo Typing, Save, and Repeat Typing.

The top menu will be updated to include the two new shortcuts. This is one of Excel's most astonishing capabilities since it allows users to easily add helpful Excel functions. This fundamental trick can be used to execute a variety of other features on the top menu.

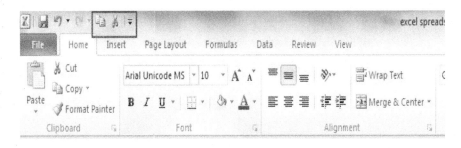

6.28 Hide Data

Most people who use Excel know how to mask data by right-clicking and selecting the Hide function. The issue is that if there is just tiny evidence of this, it can be easily noticed. Using the Format Cells feature is the simplest way to hide records entirely.

6.29 Input Restriction

This function is helpful for preserving data validity. Users frequently need to double-check input values to have guidance on the next moves. For, e.g., the date of birth on the sheet should be formatted in DD/MM/YYYY. This function works similarly to restrictions.

To ensure the data outside of this rule isn't added, go to Data->Data Validation->Setting, enter the parameters, and then switch to Input Message to send suggestions like, "Please input your date of birth in DD/MM/YYYY. When hovering the pointer over this field, users can see this post, as well as a warning message if the entered data is incorrect. The use of this function is shown in the picture below.

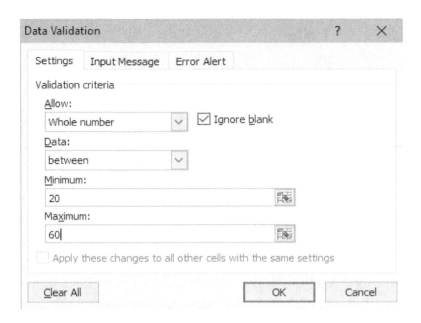

6.30 IPMT and PMT

These are one of the most relevant Excel advanced functions for users who operate in the financial industry, FP&A, real estate, or any market analyst role that deals with debt programs.

Users may use the PMT formula to calculate the worth of equivalent sums over the life of a loan. It should be used in conjunction with IPMT, which explains the payment ratios on similar loans and then divides the principal and interest amounts.

6.31 CONCATENATEX

Concatenatex works in the following way: For each row in a table, concatenates the result of the character assessment. This method takes a table or returns a table as its primary parameter.

The second parameter is a column containing the requirements you want to concatenate or a value-reflecting character.

Example

EMP table

First Name	Last Name
Elen	Smith
Janet	Ford

CONCATENATEX(Enames, [FirstName] & " " & [LastName], ",")

6.32 NETWORKDAYS

In Excel, the NETWORKDAYS feature calculates the number of working days between two dates. You may also skip defined leaves and only have working days for them. In Excel, it's referred to as a Date/Time Function.

FOR EXAMPLE, THE NUMBER OF WORKDAYS BETWEEN THE START DATE (10/10/2012) AND THE END DATE (12/10/2013) IS SHOWN IN THE EXAMPLE BELOW.

B4	▼	:	×	✓	*fx*	=NETWORKDAYS(B1,B2)		

◢	A	B	C	D	E
1	Start Date :	10/12/2012			
2	End Date :	10/12/2013			
3					
4	Number of workdays :	261			
5					

6.33 REPT

The REPT Function belongs to the category of rational functions. The role can repeat characters as many times as you want. REPT may be used to load a cell to a specific range in a market study. We can also use the feature to create histograms, a map often used in commercial modeling, by changing values in a fixed number of (iterated) instances.

This is one of Excel's most critical features. It's a popular tool in business analytics.

The string in the column [MyValue] is returned for the number of terms in the column [MyAmount] in the following sample. The output string is determined by the subject and number meaning in a row, so the process runs for the whole column.

Output

MyValue	MyAmount	ResultingColumn1
Text	3	TextTextText
Number	0	
89	3	898989

6.34 ACCRINT

For a bond that pays interest on a regular basis, the ACCRINT feature would calculate the cumulative benefit. When a safe, such as a bond, is traded or shipped to a new customer on a date other than the distribution date, ACCRINT assists consumers in determining the accumulated value.

The ACCRINT feature was added to Microsoft Excel 2007 and is not included in previous versions. Security rates are considered "clean" in economics. A bond's "clean price" excludes any benefit made before the shipping date or the most recent card charge. The amount of a security's "dirty price" includes any accumulated gain. The ACCRINT feature may be used to calculate cumulative benefits for security that conducts frequent business but keeps track of dates.

THE USAGE OF ACCRINT IS SHOWN IN THE PICTURE BELOW.

	A	B
1	Issue Date	1/01/2013
2	First Interest	1/04/2013
3	Settlement Date	1/02/2013
4	Rate	7.50%
5	Par Value	1,000
6	Frequency	4
7	Basis	2
8	Calc Method	1
9		
10	Formula	Result
11	=ACCRINT(A2,A3,A4,A5,A6,A7,A8)	6.45833
12	=ACCRINT(DATE(2013,1,15),A3,A4,A5,A6,A7,A8)	3.54167
13		
14		
15	Using the DATE function instead	
16	of referencing cell B1.	
17		

6.35 FV

The FV feature in Excel is a business function that calculates an investment's estimated value. The FV equation may be used to calculate the expected price of an asset-based on irregular, recurring payments and a set interest rate. Users can use the same units for defining valuation and Nper every time. If you have a four-year loan with a 12 % annual interest rate, you will use 12 % /12 for valuation and 4*12 for Nper.

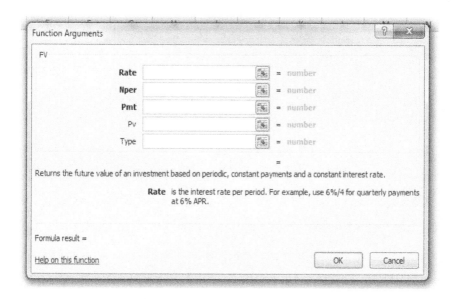

6.36 DISC function

The Discount Rate for protection is determined by the DISC feature. The day on which the security ticket is purchased or the date on which the security ticket is adjusted. The maturity date of the protection or the date on which the security ticket expires.

The following picture demonstrates how to use the DISC feature.

	Function Usage				Results	
A	B	C		A	B	C
1				1		
2	Settlement Date	42050		2	Settlement Date	2/15/2015
3	Maturity Date	42231		3	Maturity Date	8/15/2015
4	Pr	98.5		4	Pr	98.5
5	Redemption	100		5	Redemption	100
6	Basis	2		6	Basis	2
7	Discount Rate	=DISC(C2,C3,C4,C5,C6)		7	Discount Rate	2.98%

6.37 DOLLARDE

It aids in the conversion of a dollar amount seen in partial representation to a dollar amount seen in decimal representation. DOLLARDE can divide the material into sections based on an integer specified by the consumer. It's used to calculate the value of US depository bond quotes, which are estimated to the nearest 1/32 of a dollar. Since bond rates are expressed in divided dollars, the feature is handy for financial analysts when making business analyses using stock market statistics. DOLLARDE can be accessed from Microsoft Excel 2007.

THE DOLLARDE FEATURE IS DEMONSTRATED IN THE FOLLOWING PICTURE.

B1		f_x =DOLLARDE(A1,A2)		
	A	B	C	D
1	1.03	1.1875		
2	16			
3				
4				

6.38 RANDBETWEEN

This feature helps users choose a number from a pre-determined range. Excel will take the correct details from the areas to which the titles in the Range are associated and pick them after users have entered the lowest and highest numbers.

Example:

The RANDBETWEEN function is used to produce one or more random numbers in the interval between two values.

I	J
	Formula in column I
231	=RANDBETWEEN(0,300)
189	=RANDBETWEEN(0,300)
270	=RANDBETWEEN(0,300)
176	=RANDBETWEEN(0,300)
7	=RANDBETWEEN(0,300)

6.39 INDEX MATCH

An index match feature is a superior alternative to the VLOOKUP or HLOOKUP formulas, all of which have drawbacks when it comes to applying lookup employment. The INDEX MATCH is a two-functional sequencing system.

When showing and giving someone's height depending on their identification or name, for example, you may use this feature to move all variables using the INDEX MATCH.

For, e.g., we want to know how well a particular item sold for a specific region and month. The feature is a high-level version that returns a match based on a particular pattern as an output. We use the multiplication method, which also serves as the AND operator, to evaluate different steps.

`{=INDEX(D2:D13, MATCH(1, (G1=A2:A13)*(G2=B2:B13)*(G3=C2:C13), 0))}`

	A	B	C	D	E	F	G
1	Region	Month	Item	Sales		Region	North
2	North	Jan	Apples	$100		Month	Feb
3	North	Jan	Bananas	$120		Item	Apples
4	North	Feb	Apples	$115		Sales	$115
5	North	Feb	Bananas	$130			
6	North	Mar	Apples	$135			
7	North	Mar	Bananas	$125			
8	South	Jan	Apples	$110			
9	South	Jan	Bananas	$140			
10	South	Feb	Apples	$115			
11	South	Feb	Bananas	$120			
12	South	Mar	Apples	$155			
13	South	Mar	Bananas	$105			

6.40 QUARTILE

The QUARTILE function returns the quartile, or one of four equal groups, in a distributed set of data. It can return the lowest, first, second, and maximum values.

The quartile value of the cells in an arrangement is returned by this function. It also has a predictive significance based on the percentile reached. Quartiles are often used to divide populations into categories in sales and evaluation results.

For example, the QUARTILE function may be used to find the top 25% of sales in a community.

Example:

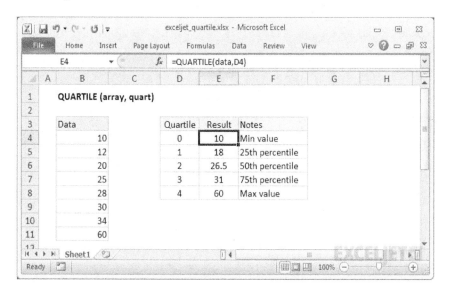

Chapter 7: Ways Excel Can Improve Your Productivity

7.1 Arranging large amounts of Data

There's a fair chance you're working with vast volumes of numbers, whether you're a data scientist or an account manager. These days, data is everywhere, and Excel is the most robust method for working with it.

Excel allows data analysis to be simple with features including pivot tables. A pivot table allows you to quickly organize and sort raw data into understandable tables by rearranging the columns. You will save time and gain strategic insights more efficiently this way.

7.2 Examining the Formulas simultaneously

Excel displays the formula instead of the outcome if you edit a cell that holds a formula. The keyboard shortcut "Control +" can be used to see all the calculations on a worksheet at once. You can alter as many formulas as you like almost instantly when you use this shortcut. It's a smart way to guarantee the consistency and fluidity of the sheet.

7.3 Automate Recurring Responsibilities with VBA

One of Excel's most useful methods is Virtual Basic of Applications (VBA). If you're used to hours of manual data entry, VBA will reduce it to only a few minutes with this simple macro. When operating at home or the hospital, this can be a big-time saver and help. Microsoft Excel is a time-saving program that will help you get a lot more done at work.

7.4 Using the Fill Handles

Most people, while applying formulas to tables, copy the formula from the 1st row of the table to the last row. You can paste a whole column of calculations with only a few keystrokes if you understand the data-navigating keyboard cutoffs in Excel. They are much faster, so you don't have to scroll to the bottom of the table.

7.5 Goal Seek Formula

Goal Seek is an Excel feature that shows you how one data element in a formula affects another. Since you can easily change a single cell entry to see the outcome, it's a handy method for answering "what if" questions. It's instrumental in economics, revenue, and predicting scenarios because it allows you to see how predictions could shift if one variable is changed.

Chapter 8: Suggestions to Improve Basic MS Excel Skills

8.1 Master the Shortcuts

You will save a lot of time by learning specific keyboard shortcuts. Even if most machine and Internet users nowadays couldn't imagine navigating online without a click, or at the very least a touchpad, using just the keyboard can save you a lot of time. Using Ctrl+c and Ctrl+v to copy and paste is typically second nature to you. Ctrl+z to reverse the previous operation, Ctrl+PgUp to move between worksheet windows, Ctrl+a to select the whole worksheet, Ctrl+F to locate objects, & Ctrl+K to add hyperlinks are several other helpful shortcuts. Microsoft has compiled a comprehensive collection of Excel keyboard shortcuts.

8.2 Import Data from a Website

It's also crucial to learn how to import data because it will significantly speed up the workflow. If you come across a website with a lot of data that you think could be useful for one of your ventures, you can transform it into a worksheet by going to File > Import External Data and then pressing New Web Query. When you press this button, a new window appears with your browser's homepage highlighted and the page's URL highlighted. Copy and paste the path to the website you want to view into the Address box. Click OK, and you're done! Your information is entered into an Excel spreadsheet.

8.3 Filter your Results

If you have a big spreadsheet with a lot of data, the best thing you can do is use the Auto filtering function. Select Data > Filter > Auto filter to do so. Using one of the small boxes, you can filter the results to meet your specific requirements.

8.4 Calculate the Sum

If you use Excel often, using shortcuts to measure the sum of an entire column or set of cells will save you a lot of time. Once you've picked the first empty cell in the list, use the shortcut Alt + = rather than manually enter the formula (the one located at the end of the numbers). After you've run this order, click Tab to see the response in Excel.

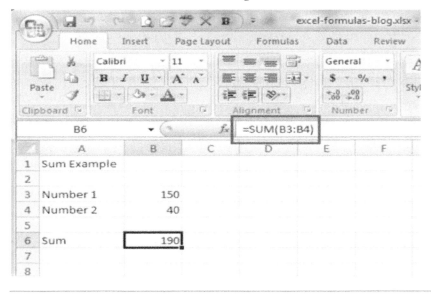

8.5 AutoCorrect and AutoFill

You can learn how to type less in Excel if you want to save more time. This can be done in two ways: AutoFill and AutoCorrect. AutoFill saves you time, mainly when manually typing in a numbered list. Go to the Edit tab, point to Fill, and then press Series to unlock it. AutoCorrect is a function that corrects misspelled words & typos automatically. To allow AutoCorrect, go to the Tools tab and pick AutoCorrect from the drop-down menu.

8.6 Display Formulas

You can switch between Excel's usual regular monitor and the display mode, which shows you how the formulas look in the method, with only a single keystroke. Ctrl + is the formula. When you press this combination once in a spreadsheet, Excel will display the formulas rather than the output of these formulas.

8.7 Manage Page Layout

You'll need to know how to handle page layout if you want your printouts to appear as impressive as the view onscreen. These choices can be found by going to the Page Layout tab. Consider experimenting with page numbering, columns, and page boundaries to see how they function before expanding.

Conclusion

The updated Excel models have all you need to get started and become a professional, as well as a wide range of valuable features. To save you time, MS Excel identifies trends and organizes results. Create spreadsheets quickly and conveniently from models or from scratch, then use modern features to conduct calculations.

It includes both basic and advanced software that can be used in almost any business environment. The Excel database helps you to build, access, update, and exchange data with others efficiently and easily. You can generate spreadsheets, data tables, data logs, budgets, and more by reading and updating excel files attached to emails. When you gain a better understanding of various definitions, you'll be able to recognize the new tools and features that Excel offers its users. The reality is that Excel functionality can accommodate almost any individual or business' needs. All you need to do is put in the effort to broaden the skills. The learning curve for developing your skills may be steep, but with practice and time, you will notice that things become second nature. After all, a person improves by repetition.

Mastering these basic Excel skills is what you need to do to make your life easier—and maybe impress those in your workplace. However, remember that no matter how familiar you are with this helpful instrument, there is always something fresh to learn. Whatever you do, keep developing your Excel skills—it will not only help you keep track of your own earnings, but it can also lead to a better potential job opportunity.

To conclude, wisdom is often said to be strong, and there's no easier way to motivate yourself than by honing your talents and the worth of your business by expertise and technology.

Printed in Great Britain
by Amazon

65899136R00088